Foreword by Darren La Croix
WORLD CHAMPION OF PUBLIC SPEAKING

Naked People Won't Help You

Keep Your Cool, Capture the Confidence, and Conquer the Fear of Public Speaking

STEVE OZER

A *Possibility Press* Book

Published by
Possibility Press
www.possibilitypress.com

Manufactured in the United States of America.

Dedication

To Mom and Dad, Harriet and Ted Ozer, on the occasion of their 50th wedding anniversary.

Acknowledgment

Despite my incredible excitement and enthusiasm about the subject matter, 180 literary agents and editors still rejected the book proposal for *Naked People Won't Help You*. However, the staff at Possibility Press immediately recognized the potential of the book and bowled me over with their energy and enthusiasm. My heartfelt thanks go to them for their warmth, spirit, and encouragement throughout the project.

A special thanks to Bill Salmon, who gave me years of encouragement and inspiration to keep on writing. I miss you every day, Bill.

Alex and Kira, you're too young to read this right now, but someday you'll see how Daddy thanked you in this book. Thanks for the laughter, the craziness, the joy, the peaches on the ceiling, the Cheerios® on the floor, the fun, and everything you've done to turn my life upside down, inside out, and everything in-between, in ways I'll cherish forever. I love you with all my heart.

"The only limit to our realization of tomorrow will be our doubts of today. Let us move forward with strong and active faith."

—Franklin D. Roosevelt

Go for It!

MANY YEARS AGO, I stood up in front of nine classmates at a public speaking phobia class in Philadelphia and delivered my first "speech." If you had been in that room, you would have seen a human being on the edge—a heart-thumping, lip-quivering, voice-quavering, head-dizzying, knee-knocking, palm-sweating, face-reddening mass of misfiring nerve endings. I could have been a heart attack in training.

Less than a year later, I stood on the stage of a theater-in-the-round, microphone in hand, and delivered a knockout, 30-minute comedy routine in front of 1,000 people at an outdoor summer festival.

This book is the result of everything that happened in-between. May all that I share enrich your life and help you make your goals and dreams a reality. Go for it!

Conquering the fear of public speaking stands as my single greatest accomplishment, and continues to bring me tremendous personal and professional rewards. When it comes to the fear that once paralyzed my life, I'm a free man; and you can be free too!"

To your success,

Steve Ozer

Contents

Foreword

What Do Naked People Have to Do with It?

OUT OF 260,000 members in 113 countries, through its over 12,800 member clubs, Toastmasters worldwide each year crowns one person the World Champion of Public Speaking. In 2001, I was fortunate enough to be that person.

When I returned home after winning the contest, I was greeted by my colleagues with praise and congratulations. The one comment that will always stand out in my mind is, "You are so lucky to have 'the gift' of speaking in front of people." My head almost exploded. Lucky? No way! Gift? Hardly! It dawned on me that this person saw only the end result. He had no idea how scared I was when I first started speaking. It was my desire to move ahead in life that drove me to do it.

Most people don't believe the fear of public speaking can be conquered. Believe me, it can. Steve Ozer, the author of this wonderful book, and I are living proof.

When I teach public speaking classes, I always show a video clip of my first time on stage, in 1992, at a Boston comedy club. I was terrible. My voice was squeaking as though I had just hit puberty. The video clearly shows the fear I had that day. In my early days of comedy, I was a wreck with stage fright for a whole week before every show. I'm still not quite sure how my friends and family put up with me.

In my 12 years on the platform, I've seen and heard many people teach public speaking, and many gave bad advice. The classic example is the old "Just picture the audience naked and you will relax." What? If I did that, I would feel just as embarrassed as if I had just walked in on someone sitting in a men's restroom stall. I would be even more anxious.

Steve Ozer has learned the art of public speaking the hard way, and he's presented his lessons well. This book is filled with inspiring real-life examples of ordinary people who overcame the fear. As you read the book, you'll know that you are not alone and that you can do it too.

Overcoming the fear of public speaking is worth everything you can do to accomplish it. Steve points out how it affects most areas of your life, from your relationship with that special someone, to reaching the pinnacle of success in your job, business, or profession.

This book gives you a step-by-step program and useful tools to conquer the fear. My favorites are Steve's Baloney Sheet and his Hierarchy of Fears. Both are potent tools you can use to soar to the top in speaking.

If you fear public speaking, follow Steve's plan. Doing so will enable you to change your life. I only wish this book had been available when I first started speaking. It would have helped me a great deal in overcoming my own fear. It would have also dramatically shortened the time it took me to really start succeeding in all areas of my life

Thank you, Steve, for this breakthrough book. I know it's going to help a lot of people.

Steve's right. Picturing people naked won't help you speak, but this book will. Read it. No, DEVOUR it! Get on the fast track to a better, richer, more rewarding life.

Much success,

Darren LaCroix

Millions of people take the fear of public speaking to their graves. They sacrifice happiness, maximum success in their careers or businesses, and ultimately their potential.

Chapter 1
Naked People Can't Help You

IMAGINE HOW YOU WOULD FEEL in the following situation: You're on the 100th floor of the Empire State Building, where you step onto an already-crowded elevator.

With a whoosh, the door closes and the elevator silently begins its descent. All of sudden, it goes into a free fall. Your stomach is in your throat. Your face goes pale. You feel a sickening knot of fear deep in your abdomen. Perspiration glistens on your forehead. Within a few seconds, the intercom crackles. The lobby guard announces, "Ladies and gentlemen, I have terrible news. The cable has snapped.... There's nothing we can do.... Your death will be relatively painless.... God bless you all.... Goodbye."

That's how I used to feel when faced even with the mere thought of public speaking. Sweating, heart racing, knees shaking, voice quavering, I'd feel dizzy and disoriented, like I was going to faint. Every nerve ending in my body sounded an alarm. Gasping for breath and gripped in a state of panic, my brain would shut down, eliminating any hope of rational thought or action.

My mother's expression was: "You could just plotz." Frankly, I was never quite sure what it meant to plotz, but I assumed it was some kind of nervous breakdown. The dictionary defines it as—"to collapse or faint as from surprise, excitement, or exhaustion, to crack, split, burst."

Whenever I anticipated speaking, I felt like I was plotzing—losing control of my emotions, and the capacity to think. For nearly two decades, I suffered from an irrational fear that nearly ruined my life. It affected my education, stunted my career options, limited my recreational activities, and suffocated me in ways I still can't believe.

For 20 years, my life was a jumble of missed opportunities, shameful avoidance, and limited career growth. The fear of public speaking haunted my waking hours and disturbed my sleep. It robbed me of confidence and hammered at my self-esteem. It exhausted me physically and mentally, and filled my waking hours with fear and anxiety. For a long time, it never dawned on me that life could be any other way.

Of course, I didn't start out plotzing. As a kid, I was playful, outgoing, and pretty normal. At eight, my parents would prop me up in front of family and friends to entertain them. My goofy jokes, silly stories, and assorted inanities would always elicit gales of laughter and healthy applause.

But the first panicky symptoms of public speaking phobia that came over me at 11 were enough to mute the laughter, muzzle the humor. It snuffed out my creativity as I avoided pubic speaking for the next 20 years. I watched in horror as those first unpleasant symptoms transformed themselves into a rat's nest of catastrophic terror, neurotic retreat, and destructive behavior.

If You Fear Public Speaking, You Are Not Alone

I found out I wasn't alone. Millions of people suffer in silence and hide in shame from this common fear. The Book of Lists cites fear of public speaking as the single greatest fear. Forty-one percent of the 3,000 people surveyed were more afraid of speaking before a group than of getting cancer! They were more afraid of it than of flying, heights, financial challenges, darkness, bugs, and even death.

The fear of public speaking is epidemic. It cuts across all demographics—from administrative professionals to aeronautical engineers, from plumbers to public figures, from cashiers to clergy, from scientists to salespeople, and from bus drivers to business owners. According to a National Comorbidity Study, 13 percent of the more than 275 million Americans will experience a social phobia, such as the fear of public speaking, during their lifetimes. That would make social phobias the third most prevalent anxiety disorder in the U.S., after depression and alcohol dependence.

CEOs to Cattle Ranchers

John Nance, president of the Speakers' Counsel, a speechwriting and coaching firm based in Denver, Colorado, has seen his share of terrified public speakers, ranging from CEOs to politicians to cattle ranchers. "The majority of my clients exhibit some of the earmarks of stage fright," says Nance. "Even those people you would assume are comfortable speaking in front of groups—like national politicians or corporate executives—suffer from the fear."

Nance comments on the diversity of people who come to him for help in overcoming the fear of public speaking. He describes one well-known politician who had no fear of public speaking until he was asked to speak at a national political convention: "Despite the fact he had given hundreds of speeches, the thought of standing on what looks like the bow of a ship, in front of 20,000 people, was absolutely terrifying to him."

In another case, there was a CEO of a Fortune 500 company who had always been comfortable speaking in front of groups. But he changed his tune when confronted with the task of communicating a major change in strategic direction to his stockholders. Another example involved a cattle rancher who, after being elected to the local school board, finally faced up to the fact that he was terrified to speak at meetings.

Why Do Many People Quietly Live with the Fear?

If so many people from all walks of life suffer from the fear of public speaking, where are the support groups and the 12-step and government programs? Where are the talk show "victims"? Why aren't more people crying out for help?

After experiencing the fear myself, and interviewing dozens of people who continue to struggle with it every day, it's clear most people just resign themselves to living with it. They're not sharing their plight on "The Oprah Winfrey Show." They don't write to their elected officials about it. They don't form support groups or seek out professional help.

There are five main reasons why people continue to live with the fear of public speaking:

Reason #1: They're ashamed.
Reason #2: They feel better avoiding it.
Reason #3: They believe they're alone.
Reason #4: They believe there's no cure.
Reason #5: They listen to questionable advice.

Let's explore them one at a time:

Reason #1—They're ashamed. Just as I suffered silently for nearly 20 years, most people who are terrified of public speaking don't talk about it. They are concerned about what others think of them, and are mortified at the thought of appearing weak or incompetent. So, to appear confident and in control, they often mask inner turmoil beneath a facade of self-confidence, firm handshakes, and can-do attitudes. They weave tightly knit cocoons around their fears, safely tucking them away from family, friends, colleagues, and associates.

Ironically, those terrified of public speaking are often exceptionally talented. They can be brilliant businesspeople, effective networkers, beloved public servants, empathetic counselors, successful entrepreneurs—even heads of major corporations and other industry leaders. They are people you would least expect to be afraid. One-on-one, they can dazzle you with eloquent conviction. At social gatherings, they can charm with panache. But in front of an audience, a strange metamorphosis occurs—the confidence dissolves, the charm withers, and the shell cracks. Left behind is a frightened, quivering, and ashamed person with public-speaking phobia.

Reason #2—They feel better avoiding it. When someone who's afraid of public speaking even thinks about it, he or she may feel like a "basket case." The act of avoiding it can bring immediate relief—but may have serious long-term consequences.

Take Jack for example. A bright, articulate man in his 40s, he is a prime example of why some people choose to live with the fear of public speaking. Jack believed his purpose in life was to help people. Fresh out of college at 21, he set his sights on a career in social services. He knew it wouldn't pay well, but he felt it would give him the satisfaction of using his knowledge and people skills in ser-vice to others.

Eventually Jack was hired as a counselor at an agency that helps troubled adolescents; it was a dream come true. He was doing what he was trained for and, more important, he loved it. Being compassionate, he felt very sad about the families' lives and living conditions of the kids he counseled. Nonetheless, he was confident in his capacity to help. He had chosen the right profession. Jack excelled as a counselor and soon made his mark on the agency. His family marveled at his eagerness to go to work in the morning, and at his energy and enthusiasm when he got home. Jack loved his job, and it showed.

But, regardless of appearances, all wasn't well with Jack. Secretly, he harbored a tremendous fear of public speaking.

Early on in his job, it wasn't an issue, because he just dealt with people one-on-one. Whether he was counseling a troubled teenager or discussing a case with his supervisor, Jack was an excellent communicator—passionate, articulate, reasoned, and confident. But when the agency instituted weekly meetings for counselors to share their case studies and compare notes, things began to unravel.

Jack was terrified. At the first meeting, as he watched his associates gather in the conference room, chatting amiably and filling their coffee cups, he felt a sickening lump in his throat. His heart raced. His mouth was dry. He felt light-headed and gasped for breath. After everyone was seated, the supervisor asked each counselor to spend five minutes updating the group on the most challenging cases.

Jack sweated profusely beneath his sport coat. His head throbbed and his hands shook uncontrollably. Finally, it was his turn. With a quavering, barely audible voice, he talked for about 60 seconds before trailing off mid-sentence. Then it was on to the next counselor.

Jack was devastated. Although no one seemed to be complaining about his report, he was sure his career had ended in that conference room. He was concerned that people could see he was weak, helpless, insecure, and even a discredit to his profession. Surely, he thought, whatever confidence his boss had in him until that point must have vanished with his pathetic 60-second performance. In Jack's mind, he was a stone-dead loser.

Jack continued to shine as a counselor in his individual sessions. However, when he found himself stuck in that conference room every week, he dreaded his turn to speak. He fought dry mouth, and had a quavering voice as he would barely squeak out his report.

Finally, he could take the anguish no more. After months of suffering in silence at the weekly meetings, Jack resigned from his job. In doing so, he no longer had to endure the panic and anxiety of these meetings. He was free.

But that freedom carried a heavy price. By avoiding his most dreaded fear, Jack had quit the profession he so desperately loved. Distraught, and filled with a deepening sense of gloom, he sought out a job where he would not have to talk to any group—a job where he would be left alone to carry out his duties. He found a position as a mail carrier. Unfortunately, this story does not have a happy ending. Today, Jack hates his job, himself, and the way he treats his family after each long, weary day at work.

Like many people who develop a phobia about public speaking, Jack chose avoidance as the antidote to his poisonous fear. By avoiding a job which required him to speak in front of groups, he felt physical and mental relief. He had found the lure of a panic-free existence simply too tempting an escape to let reason stand in the way.

Avoidance, however, became a double-edged sword. It brought him welcome relief from the anxiety and, in this sense, removed him from "harm's way." But, over time, he began to attach even greater significance and consequence to his fear that was already blown out of proportion. So, was he really any better off? Hardly.

Sally also found temporary relief through avoidance. At 39, she seemed the epitome of the successful career woman. As a customer service manager for a major pharmaceutical firm, Sally was smart, competent, outgoing, and focused on success. She was confident, aggressive, and even tough. But beneath that facade beat the heart of a woman in mortal fear of public speaking.

"I had an absolutely terrifying experience in church when I was 17," she remembers. "Every Sunday, I would sing in the choir, and feel comfortable in front of a large audience, because I was part of a group. One Sunday, however, our soloist called out sick, and I was chosen to be her replacement. I was mortified. I felt sick to my stomach. I was in a panic. But I did everything I could to hide the fear.

"When it came time for me to sing solo, I froze in place. I couldn't make a sound. I was absolutely terrified and totally embarrassed. Somehow, though, the choir managed to stumble forward without me. And when the services ended that Sunday, I went home totally humiliated."

Today, more than 20 years later, Sally still associates "performing" before a large group of people with panic, anxiety, and humiliation. It's been a rocky road. "After being with my company for five years, I was promoted to administrative assistant to the president," she recalls.

"In that position, I was responsible for presenting employee safety statistics to the company's executive committee. It was a terrifying responsibility, not only because I had to speak in front of a group, but because the group was so powerful. I had seen the way this group tore into each other, and I could only imagine what they would do to me. I thought they would eat me alive."

She recalled those sessions with acute discomfort. "My hands would be shaking and my knees knocking," she says shuddering. "And I would insist on sitting, rather than standing. My voice would be quavering, and the only way I could get through it was to remember that I was speaking on behalf of all our employees, that I had an obligation to do it." Although Sally made it through each presentation intact, she found it an agonizing experience and loathed to repeat it.

She admits that she has avoided opportunities for advancement because of her fear. "I've turned down positions in marketing research, sales, and public affairs," she laments. "Although I knew I had the skills for those jobs, I knew each of them involved some amount of public speaking, and I just couldn't handle that."

Sally confesses she's used her creative energy to avoid speaking before groups. "I remember when my boss asked me to make a presentation to a group of customers on the subject of our company's cash management practices," she says. "But I didn't just try to avoid it, I actively campaigned against it. I argued with my boss that it was a terrible idea—that it would be airing our dirty laundry in public. I was very convincing and, in the end, he canceled the session."

Sally has used other techniques to get out of public speaking and one, in particular, is very effective for her. "I'll charm someone else into doing a presentation," she says mischievously. "I'll make them think it was their idea to do it, that they would be perfect for the assignment. To be honest, I don't feel like I'm being deceptive. I give 150 percent to my company in other ways, so I don't feel so bad."

Is she being dishonest? Has she compromised her integrity to avoid public speaking? Unfortunately, she and many others are doing just that—in their efforts to dodge speaking responsibilities. Perhaps you are among these people. If Sally looks at her behavior truthfully, she may realize it's time to stop playing the games and look for help in conquering her fear. The challenge is that people like Sally often don't believe they can be helped. Since avoidance is such a big factor in holding people back from speaking, we'll cover it in depth in Chapter 4.

Reason #3—They believe they're alone. Sally's story is not unique. People who have developed a fear of public speaking believe they are alone, and invest an incredible amount of energy in hiding their predicament. To make matters worse, they are surrounded by people who seem to be comfortable at public speaking—their bosses, associates, colleagues, friends, and family members. Even people interviewed on the street during TV news programs seem comfortable, confident, and at ease in giving their opinions in front of thousands of viewers.

For the person with public-speaking phobia, everyone else seems well-adjusted. They are misinterpreting what may be false fronts of bravado, with their own quaking insides, probably covered by their own falsely projected self-assurance. Believing others have it all together only makes them feel even more ashamed, helpless, and incompetent. They need to remember all people are not as they appear—by far.

Kevin, 63, is someone who knows what it's like to feel alone, to carry the shame of his speaking phobia with him every day. Now a retired police chief in Florida, Kevin remembers the anxiety and helplessness he felt when he first experienced the fear of public speaking at 22.

"I was a narcotics officer, involved in physically dangerous situations every day," he recalls. "But nothing compared to the time I was asked to speak in front of a group of 300 doctors on the subject of 'Drugs on the Street.' From the moment I was asked to speak, I became completely distracted from my regular life. I couldn't sleep, eat, or think straight. I suffered anxiety every day for three weeks before the event.

When the dreaded day finally came, I was a nervous wreck. The event was held at a fancy hotel, and I had to get up in front of a huge audience in an auditorium. Staring out at the sea of people, I was completely intimidated. I couldn't catch my breath, and I found it extremely difficult to get even the first word out." Out of sheer panic, Kevin decided to scrap the talk and simply take questions from the audience. Although he managed to get through it, he left the hotel embarrassed and ashamed.

Many years later, Kevin managed to contain his fear and was eventually able to make presentations without panicking. But unfortunately, the fear came rushing back. "I was a police chief by then, and I was called upon to make many presentations," he remembers. "Some of them were to angry crowds, and that's where all of the anxiety would return. I started bringing other police officers with me to these presentations, and I would point to one of them to handle the questions. Pretty soon, I was delegating the talks to other officers; I avoided them altogether."

Three months after completely avoiding his first talk, Kevin suffered a nervous breakdown, part of which he attributes to the fear of public speaking. He has since retired, and has written two novels. "I really enjoy being a writer, but I am a little nervous that if my books sell and become successful, it will force me to do some public speaking." At 63, Kevin still remains a prisoner of his fear.

Thousands of people like Kevin take the fear of public speaking to their graves. In doing so, they sacrifice their self-esteem, careers or businesses, and their ultimate potential for success.

Reason #4—They believe there's no cure. You can be cured. If I had known that 20 years ago, I would have had hope, seen a way out, and spared myself the paranoia, terror, anxiety, and helplessness that came from this life-altering phobia. But, at that time, I believed as thousands of others do today, that the fear of public speaking is incurable. I used to believe it was a sad twist of fate. It seemed to be almost a cruel joke that someone like me, who was so outgoing, energetic, and filled with enthusiasm for work and play could be locked inside four walls of fear.

Twenty years ago, I would have given anything to have had the confidence to get up in front of an audience, to make them laugh, cry, and move them to take action. At every meeting, every class, every gathering, I would look at each speaker with a sense of awe and envy. I wanted to do what they could do, with every bone in my body. But I had resigned myself to a life spent among the audience—not in front of it.

If only I had met someone who had actually conquered the fear, I might have found hope. I knew people who had overcome the fear of flying. I saw people on television who had been victorious over the fear of driving. I even knew someone who had triumphed over the fear of snakes. But never did I read, see, or hear about anyone who had faced up to the fear of public speaking and conquered it forever.

Today, I'm paid to give speeches in front of software designers, communications professionals, newspaper editors, police officers, entrepreneurs, and thousands of others. I've performed stand-up comedy in nightclubs, amphitheaters, and auditoriums. I've spoken in front of enormous crowds, and I have been hired to speak to dozens of large gatherings at conferences, banquets, meetings, and conventions.

Although I still experience "butterflies," i.e., a little nervousness before speaking, frankly it helps keep me sharp. I have won out over my old fear of public speaking once and for all. I no longer dread it, lose my appetite weeks before a speech, or suffer from overwhelming anxiety at the mere thought of facing a group.

Now, I actually look forward to speaking in front of groups. It's restored my sense of confidence, repaired my self-esteem, and given me a life I never knew I could have. Today, conquering the fear of public speaking stands as my single greatest accomplishment, and continues to bring me tremendous personal and professional rewards. When it comes to the fear that once paralyzed my life, I'm a free man and you can be free too.

Overcoming the fear of public speaking has also given me the opportunity to bring hope to people who are still trapped by their fear. In my presentations to corporations, business owners, professional organizations, civic groups, and others, I've talked candidly about my struggle to overcome the fear of public speaking, and how it has dramatically transformed my life. In doing so, it seems I've broken an unspoken taboo—talking about personal weakness and emotional challenges in the business world.

No matter how enlightened an organization is today, it still seems that, by and large, we are expected to have consistent emotional strength in business without consideration for human frailties. In many cases, we're expected to check our feelings and emotions at the door, put on a mask of confidence and competence with our colleagues, associates, and leaders, and appear strong at all times.

In my presentations, I'm always amazed to hear business people open up about their fears, and voice the embarrassment and shame they've lived with for so many years. It reminds me of how hard it was for me to hide my fears from my colleagues, to appear upbeat and in control, week after week, but secretly dreading the day I would be exposed for my weakness.

Reason #5—They listen to questionable advice. I feel uncomfortable telling you this, but I did at least one really stupid thing when I first endeavored to conquer my fear. I made a doctor's appointment at a local medical center where several doctors work together. The physicians there participate in an HMO and their facility was set up much like my bank. In the waiting room, patients were lined up in single file between two velvet ropes that snaked through the office up to a nurse's station. When I got to the front of the line, the nurse escorted me to see whichever doctor was available at the time—not necessarily an appropriate one. For example, the first time I went, I saw a gynecologist!

After awkwardly telling the doctor about my fear of public speaking, he recommended two things: 1) "Relax!" and 2) Take some heart medication to slow down my heart rate. Frankly, I would have lost all confidence in this doctor had it not been for his progressive office policy: If you die at any time during the course of treatment, he cheerfully refunds your five-dollar co-payment!

I'm joking here. But perhaps the greatest tragedy for those who suffer from the fear of public speaking is this: When you eventually reach the breaking point, and you finally get the courage to turn for help, instead of finding the compassion, support, and guidance you need, you are often met with well-intentioned—but questionable—advice.

Psychiatrists generally want to spend years probing your child- hood history, scouring your psyche for the parental relationships that may have laid the foundation for the anxiety. Family doctors often treat only the symptoms, prescribing magic pills from their pharmaceutical arsenals. The most unfortunate part is that these and other certainly well-intentioned but perhaps uninformed professionals often reinforce the belief that there is no cure. The sad irony, perhaps unbeknownst to these caregivers, is that the fear of public speaking is a very treatable disorder.

People who turn to published experts may not fare much better. Books written on public speaking tend to concentrate on speaking techniques rather than on ways to conquer fear. Often, they stress preparation as the antidote to anxiety. Concentrate on what you are going to say, they tell you, and your fears will magically disappear.

One author claims he cured a lifelong fear of public speaking by spending a weekend preparing for a speech. Preparation is certainly key to effective public speaking. Yet, unless your fear is totally based on your concern about not being prepared, preparation is not going to be the cure-all.

Another author espouses three secrets to banishing the fear of public speaking: 1) Know your subject; 2) Believe in your subject; and 3) Practice, practice, practice.

Still another author recommends three fear-reducing activities to do before giving a speech: 1) Walking around the block; 2) Waggling your jaw back and forth; and 3) Dangling your arms at your sides. To be honest, I've walked, waggled, and dangled, and none of it did anything to help me speak in public.

But my all-time favorite piece of traditional but utterly useless advice essentially claims that you'll be relaxed and able to speak with confidence by picturing your audience without a stitch of clothes on. But if there's one thing I've learned in nearly 20 years of trial and error, it is this—imagining the people in your audience as being naked won't help you! I'm sorry, it just won't.

Your audience may fill the auditorium with all the naked splendor you could possibly imagine, but your thinking of them as being naked and, therefore, supposedly un-intimidating, won't help you speak with any degree of confidence. In your mind you may imagine them giving you their undivided, unclothed attention. In your mind you may even imagine them nodding approvingly, wearing nothing more than the hair on their head and a smile. But in the end, all that imagery simply won't help you speak to them!

What will help you, however, is understanding why you're so scared in the first place, along with a step-by-step plan to conquer the fear of public speaking forever. Part I of this book gives you the understanding. Part II gives you the plan.

I still look back in amazement at the road I traveled to overcome this common fear. I unloaded my troubles onto psychologists. I put my faith in hypnotists. I read dozens of books and hundreds of articles. But nowhere did I see a clear path out of my anxiety.

However, through a combination of self-study, group therapy, trial and error, and sheer dumb luck, I managed to conquer the fear of public speaking and turn my life around. In doing so, I uncovered the facts and fallacies that surround this common fear, and the methods that work, and those that don't, in overcoming it.

Naked People Won't Help You is the result of my experiences. I see it as my chance to give back to others what I so desperately craved 15 years ago. It's written for those whose fear of public speaking has drastically or even somewhat affected the quality of their lives. It's for people who think they are alone. It's for those who have looked for help but have lost all hope. It's for people who want to help others overcome this fear. And it is for those who don't want to go to their graves thinking how it might have been.

For 20 years, I was like an early color TV with the switch set to black and white. I knew that if I could just flip the magical switch to conquer the fear of public speaking, I'd show the world a rainbow of colors. If I can conquer the fear of public speaking, I'm 100 percent positive you can do it too.

Chapter 2
Naked and Back Again—My Story

TO THIS DAY, I still chuckle about some of the ridiculous stories my father used to make up when I was little. My brothers and I don't know what to make of the one about our black-and-white television that magically transformed itself into color at the flip of a mysteriously placed switch.

Back in the early 1960s, it seemed as though our family was the only one on the block with a black-and-white television. All of our neighbors had glorious living color. To three little boys growing up in Chester, Pennsylvania, it seemed like "The Wonderful World of Disney" on Sunday nights was just a little less wonderful in various shades of gray.

Of course, we always complained about it to Dad as he was sitting in his recliner trying to read the newspaper. Occasionally he'd nod sympathetically, or he would give us another sign he wasn't really paying attention. Finally one night, after badgering him for about ten minutes, he said to us very casually from behind the paper, "You know, that actually is a color television."

"That is not a color television—it's black and white!" we screamed back.

Dad put down his newspaper with a sigh of exasperation.

"Actually, I never told you this, but there's a switch on the back of the TV that changes it to color. I just haven't had the chance to get back there and do it."

"Flip the switch!" we screamed at him like wild banshees.

"I'm too tired tonight," Dad said, burying his head back in the paper. "Maybe tomorrow night."

Coincidentally, this was the first childhood memory all three of us confided in our therapists later in life.

Flip My Switch, Please

For 20 years, I was like the color TV with the switch set to black and white. I knew that if I could just flip the magical switch to conquer the fear of public speaking, I'd show the world a rain- bow of colors. But for nearly two decades, that switch was as elusive as the one the three little boys searched for so desperately, on the back of the Zenith console, back in 1962.

I wasn't afraid of public speaking at all until I was 11. Before that, my parents had no shame in turning me into a mini-Al Jolson to act out skits, tell jokes, and sing songs in front of family and friends. I was clearly a ham. But that changed in the sixth grade when my kindly teacher, Mrs. Dodd, with her oval glasses and blondish-gray hair, called me up in front of the class to give an oral book report.

As I stood there facing my classmates, for the first time in my short little life, waves of panic overtook me. I was paralyzed with fear...I tried to speak...but the words just wouldn't come out...nothing. Seconds went by...and soon my classmates began to giggle nervously, then laugh out loud. Finally, Mrs. Dodd suggested that the mute little boy sit down and try it again another day.

Back then, I couldn't even spell the word humiliated, but that's how I felt. I sat down and said to myself with as much certainty as an 11-year-old could muster, "I will never stand up in front of other people again. I will never get those feelings again. I will never lose my voice again, not for as long as I live!" I was passionate about avoiding that experience. Over the next 20 years, I would prove to myself just how much I meant those words.

I never made that oral book report. On the next day I was scheduled to get up in front of the class, but I woke up with a mysterious stomach ailment. So, instead of facing a classroom filled with kids laughing at me, I spent the day on the sofa covered in blankets.

As I watched television (I could live with the black and white), Mom was bringing me chicken soup. By avoiding having to speak in front of my class, I felt no feelings of panic, no sense of embarrassment, no public humiliation. It was the first time I would associate avoidance with comfort, and it was an association that would help me and haunt me for the next two decades.

I became incredibly good at avoiding public speaking. Somehow I managed to get through all my years of school and college without facing a group. During that period, two things were happening simultaneously that turned out to be contradictory. First, I was becoming the class clown. I was the kid sitting in the back of the room, hurling one-liners at inappropriate times, imitating Jerry Lewis on the in-house television system, and making fun of the cafeteria menu on the school intercom. I was getting laughs. And I loved it.

But at the same time, I was developing a greater fear of public speaking. Terror was building inside of me. The more people saw me as funny and entertaining, the more terrified I became. I just knew I couldn't show my funny side in front of an audience.

Every fall, for example, the senior class of my high school put on a talent show, called "The Follies," which drew a huge audience to the auditorium over several nights. I came up with the idea of doing a large-scale parody of "The Tonight Show," Starring Johnny Carson. After putting together a group of kids to work on the idea, we had our first meeting. When someone suggested I play Johnny Carson, I froze at the thought. My head started pounding. I felt nauseous and was making myself dizzy just thinking of the idea of me doing a stand-up comedy routine in front of 500 people. I believed that there was no way I could do it, so I pushed forcefully for someone else to play Johnny. I argued that I needed to spend my time writing the jokes and other routines for the skit. It worked.

On opening night, I sat in the audience with 499 other people and watched as someone else took center stage and told my jokes, and listened as the auditorium roared with laughter. I realized from that point on I would always experience life from the sidelines—I would have to channel any talent I had through other people. I was struck with an overwhelming sense of sadness at the thought. Nonetheless, I was prepared to live with it for the rest of my life.

Avoiding public speaking got a little trickier in college, but I still managed to pull it off. Some classes did require oral presentations, but I wouldn't know it until I showed up for them. So, on the first day of each class, I would quickly scan the syllabus and see if there was an oral presentation required. If there was, I would wait for the class to end, then head over to the administration building and drop it. At the end of four years, I amazingly received my degree without making even one presentation!

Behind all my successful avoidance, however, the fear was turning into a monster. It was becoming a terrifying, menacing, all-consuming paranoia. I was totally preoccupied with it, and it had become completely irrational. I was petrified at the mere thought of public speaking, let alone doing it. If I found myself in a situation in which there was even the slightest chance that I might have to do it, my body would go into a panic mode. My heart would pound like a jackhammer. My pulse would race. My face would turn deathly pale. I'd shake uncontrollably and sweat profusely.

To put it plainly, I'd go out of control. And that's the baggage I took with me into the working world.

Fear Goes to Work

In 1980, I was hired as a communications specialist at a then- local Philadelphia bank, where I received my first taste of corporate life. At 23, I was bursting with curiosity and ambition. I was ready to take on the world, as long as I didn't have to speak to a group about it. And I made sure I didn't. I was mute at staff meetings, silent at team meetings, and avoided even the smallest of presentations. I was still seen as an enthusiastic and outgoing employee, one who was persuasive and excelled at one-on-one conversation. But I always hid the fear behind an ever-present smile and a firm handshake.

I didn't realize how I had let the fear of public speaking take control of my life. In 1981, I left the bank and accepted a job with a computer company. I couldn't resist the glamorous opportunity and the once outrageous salary offer of $17,000. But there was also a knot in the pit of my stomach about what would lie ahead.

As my first day of work approached, I became consumed with a general sense of anxiety. Subconsciously, I was saying to myself, "Will I still be able to avoid public speaking in this job?" "Will my days of hiding the fear come to an end?" "Will I finally be exposed as a fraud?"

I didn't have to worry for long, because I quit my job on the first day! At the time, I told myself the company was completely disorganized. No one knew who I was when I showed up, and besides, I was herded like a head of cattle into a room with a dozen other young marketing writers and given nothing to do. Baloney! I really quit because the fear of public speaking had overtaken me, and I was now terrified of any new unfamiliar situation.

With my tail between my legs, I asked for my old job back at the bank. Fortunately, they rehired me. However, about six months later, I left again, this time for a job with a company that sold collectible dinner plates, dolls, and other such items. I felt that generalized sense of anxiety as the first day on the job approached. I was more anxious than when I had gone to the computer company. I didn't realize that the fear of public speaking was, once again, taking over my subconscious thoughts, as I made myself a nervous wreck.

On my first day at the collectibles company, I was overcome with anxiety and had trouble concentrating on what anyone was saying to me. I remember blindly filling out a bunch of forms in personnel, being escorted to my small office and spending the rest of that first day pretending to read company literature.

The next three days at my new job were more of the same. I sat in my office filled with a sense of impending dread. When someone would stop by to welcome me or say hello, I responded enthusiastically, but in my heart I was crying out with fear of what might come next. Sitting in my office on the fourth day, I noticed a few papers in my in-box, and I took them out and glanced down at the first one. It was a memorandum from the vice president of my department talking about the upcoming staff meeting and mentioning my role at that meeting.

I panicked. My heart started pounding. I broke out in a cold sweat. My vision blurred. My knees began shaking uncontrollably. I had to get out of my office. I had to get out of the building. I had to get out of the company. Gripped with fear, I stood up, walked out of my office, went down the hallway, and out the front door—never to return.

I was still living with my parents at the time, and I surely had trouble explaining this one to them. Six months earlier, I had quit a new job on the first day; now I had quit another new job after four days. I worked hard at giving them some good, sound reasons why I could not tolerate the company. But these excuses hung in the room with the faint air of desperation and humiliation. My parents were worried;

something clearly was wrong, and they didn't think it was my choice of companies. But they were baffled as to why I would throw away two good jobs on what appeared to be a whim. Eventually, we dropped the subject. We all hoped the unpleasantness of the situation would fade over time.

Once again, I asked for my old job back at the bank. This time, though, they declined.

Help Wanted—Anxiety-Free Employment

By the time I landed my next substantial job in 1982, with a chemical firm, I knew I needed help before I even got started. My parents still didn't know what had happened at my last two jobs. But they knew I needed to find a way to get through the heebie-jeebies of that first week—without bolting at the first sign of anxiety.

My father urged me to go to the doctor and get a prescription for a stress relief medication, one that would keep me relatively calm while I adjusted to my new surroundings. I didn't like the idea of relying on drugs, but I did it anyway, filling a prescription for a sedative, in anticipation of my first day.

I remember Dad driving me into the city on that first day of work. My head was floating with the effects of the medication, and I was concerned about how to get through those first eight hours of the new job. I wasn't exactly clearheaded, but I wasn't panic stricken either. It wasn't long before I managed to get accustomed to my surroundings, and after one week, I stopped taking the medicine. I chose to stay at this great company and still worked there after 20 years.

True to form, I continued to "bob and weave" for several more years when it came to public speaking at my new company. I al- ways found a way to shift the attention to somebody else at a staff meeting, to get someone else to make a team presentation, or to avoid a speech at a public relations conference. I also knew that this behavior couldn't go on forever. It was going to catch up with me. If I didn't deal with my obsessive fear, my career at this fine company would eventually come to a crashing halt. But how much longer could I get away with it? One year? Three years? Five years?

I never found out. I was about to have an experience that would force me to confront my fears head on—one that would put me face to face with my future.

A Chip off the Old Block

My father had worked for an aircraft manufacturing company for 37 years before announcing his retirement. And for all of those years, Ted Ozer had been plagued with a debilitating fear of public speaking. It wasn't that big a deal early in his career when he worked as a machinist. But after a series of promotions over many years, he eventually became a design engineer, a job which required him to make presentations from time to time.

Dad was terrified by the prospect of making those talks. On the night before a presentation, he would pace the floors and rub his hands together, while his face became pale and etched with anxiety. My mother would do her best to calm his fears, telling him what a good job he would do, assuring him that everything would be fine. But in the end, it seemed to be a hopeless task. My father had suffered from the fear of public speaking for decades. And that fear would continue through the day he retired at 60.

His retirement party had shaped up to be a gala affair. After so many years there, Dad's career had touched a lot of people. On the night of his retirement dinner, more than 100 colleagues, friends, and family members were invited to attend the party at a local hotel. I still remember how festive the atmosphere was. Colleague after colleague came up to the podium to pay tribute to my father for his many years of exceptional contributions.

I was sitting with our family at a table near the front of the room, carefully watching my dad as he listened to all of the tributes and applause. He was slowly sinking....

My father was dreading going up to the podium at the end of the evening to make a speech. Here he was at the culmination of his career, at a time when he deserved to be basking in the glow of appreciation. Instead, he was overcome with fear. He looked haggard, pale, and disoriented. He would rather have been anywhere else than in that room.

I knew how he felt. Boy, did I know how he felt! I thought, "What could I possibly do for him now—for a man who has suffered something so painful for so long? What could I possibly do?"

So I gave him some encouragement—"Dad, you can do it." He felt just a little bit better. I then encouraged him more—"Dad, the people love you and want to hear from you. Just tell them what's in your heart." He felt considerably better. And finally, after three hearty votes of encouragement, my father got up there behind the podium and somehow, though haltingly and nervously, made it through the speech.

I have to admit, for a minute I considered how I could take someone positive with me to cheer me on everywhere I went, just in case I'd be asked to speak in front of a group. But nah, that definitely wasn't feasible.

Watching my father go through this ordeal at his retirement party was the moment of truth for me. That's when I said to myself,

"I am not going to sit at my retirement party, 15 to 20 years from now, consumed with fear because I have to make a speech at the end of the evening. I am not going to spend the next 15 to 20 years in pain. I'm going to do something about it, and I'm going to do something about it now! I was scared. I had no idea how I was going to do it. But today, I told myself, I'm putting a stake in the ground with the following message: "I will conquer the fear of public speaking if it's the last thing I do!"

The first thing I needed to do was get smart. I knew nothing about the adventure I was about to embark on. So, I went out and bought every book I could find on fighting fear, conquering phobias, and becoming a competent public speaker. I went to the library and searched for relevant magazine articles, microfiche (there was no Internet back then), and books I might have missed.

I amassed this enormous pile of information and spent weeks pouring through it. But by the time I was done, I was disappointed. There was very little, if anything, on conquering public-speaking phobias. There was a paragraph here, and a chapter there, but very little that talked about the mind-numbing, white-knuckled fear that secretly destroys lives. (Mental note to myself—write a book about this when you're done.) As you'll learn, some of the advice I managed to find was not particularly useful.

A Ray of Hope

It all seemed hopeless until December 1996, when something in a local newspaper caught my eye—an ad promoting a ten-week clinic for people suffering from public-speaking phobias. I couldn't believe my eyes! This was exactly what I had been looking for. I called the number listed for Temple University Hospital and eagerly gave them my name. The clinic started one month later, in January 1997.

The next ten weeks would change my life. The clinic was taught by Dr. Julie Weiss, a Philadelphia psychologist who specializes in helping people with public-speaking phobias. On the first night of class, I was amazed she had somehow managed to corral ten petrified people into a room. Like me, these were people who had spent a lifetime avoiding public speaking. They, too, were terrified at the prospect of standing up in front of the group.

For the first exercise, Dr. Weiss called me to the front of the room. Standing behind me as I faced the group, she explained that this exercise would be to simply stand in front of the group and say nothing. I looked out at the other nine people, and was sure my legs were going to buckle. As the seconds went by, my heart was going pound, pound, pound—seemingly ready to burst out of my chest.

But Dr. Weiss asked me to continue standing there, while looking at the audience, and saying nothing. She said to take deep breaths through my nose and allow my body sensations to just happen, rather than fight them.

She reassuringly pointed out that my heart could not keep pounding that hard for very long. She was right. After a few seconds, the pounding slowed down a bit. Then it slowed even more. Finally, as I continued to face the audience, my heart was beating somewhat faster than normal, but it wasn't what I would call pounding. For the first time in my life, I was looking out at an audience without the fear of an impending heart attack.

For the next exercise, she had each one of us go to the front of the room to say one short, positive statement. Then she had us say two sentences, and sit down. Then one short paragraph, and so on.

She talked about how the things we tell ourselves subconsciously have a profound effect on our comfort level in front of a group. She shared about how we all tend to be self-critical before an audience and why so many of us see public speaking as such a high-risk activity. Dr. Weiss deftly employed a combination of simple, but powerful, behavioral exercises. She gave us a greater understanding of our psychological makeup, and how to affect a tremendous amount of change in a short period of time.

The results were dramatic. On the first day, all of our hearts pounded as we stood silently in front of the class. Ten weeks later, each of us gave a ten-minute speech to a room full of classmates, friends, and invited guests. While I had made remarkable progress, I knew I wasn't quite yet cured.

Enter Toastmasters

I was astonished at my ability to talk in front of the phobia class. But I was also concerned that the course was coming to an end. I knew that the only way to lock in a cure was to find a way to speak in front of people as often as possible. That's when I began to think about a group I had heard about in the past—Toastmasters International. I didn't know exactly what Toastmasters was, but I was about to find out what a fine organization it is.

As you'll learn much more about later, Toastmasters is a non-profit organization, with local clubs around the world, dedicated to the art of public speaking. Members from all walks of life come together, anywhere from once a week to once a month, to practice public speaking in a safe, comfortable, non-threatening environment.

Toastmaster meetings follow a certain format, including sections dedicated to spontaneous speaking exercises, formal speeches, individual evaluations, and more. Someone at work gave me the phone number for Toastmasters' International headquarters in California, and told me to call and request a computerized printout of clubs in my area. Another way to get information on Toastmasters is to visit their website: www.toastmasters.org.

Sure enough, there was a club that met just a short distance from my house. I was nervous as a tick when I showed up for my first Toastmasters meeting. I found a group of professionals chatting casually with each other, and it was obvious that everyone was extremely comfortable with the setting and with one another. "I'm Roy Beatty," said one particularly friendly man who came up to me, offering me his hand. "Welcome to Toastmasters."

Much to my surprise, I was swept into the group and became a full-fledged Toastmaster before I knew it. Every week, I was called upon to speak spontaneously during the "Table Topics" portion of the meeting. I progressed through the Toastmasters' manual, giving formal speeches with objectives such as showing vocal variety and inspiring the audience. I listened carefully as my speeches were evaluated by experienced members of the group.

As I attended Toastmasters week after week, a remarkable thing happened—I began to see my anxiety level go down bit by bit. And I felt my comfort level start to rise bit by bit. I even started to practice some more advanced aspects of public speaking, like hand gestures, vocal variety, and body language. I began winning first place ribbons for my formal speeches. I started seeing what effect my sense of humor could have on an audience. I also started developing an emerging public speaking style that was truly my own. But I still knew I wasn't cured...yet.

Taking It on the Road

I had no doubt I would eventually become comfortable speaking in front of the same small group week after week, especially with people I had come to know and like. However, I felt I wouldn't be cured officially of the fear of public speaking until I had spoken to a group of complete strangers—outside of Toastmasters.

Could I find the courage to face an outside group? Could I bear to hear someone introduce me to a group, then walk myself to the front of the room on sound footing, give an interesting presentation, and say thank you? Did I have the nerve? I soon found out.

I called the program chairman of a local Rotary Club to see if the group had any interest in hearing a presentation on "Conquering the Fear of Public Speaking." The chairman was only slightly suspicious until I apparently answered his two questions satisfactorily: "Was the presentation free?" and "Was I trying to sell something?" My yes and no were apparently the right answers.

I must admit I was scared when I showed up at the restaurant where the Rotary meeting was held. I didn't know how many people would be there; but it didn't really matter. This was a seminal moment for me because it would prove once and for all whether I had conquered the fear of public speaking. Not sure where the meeting room was, I went up to a woman with a clipboard who was seating people in the restaurant.

"Can you tell me where the Rotary meeting is?" I said, betraying just a hint of anxiousness in my voice.

"Oh, they're sitting over there," she replied, obviously bored with her job. She then pointed to a small group of men sitting in the restaurant.

Sure enough, there were six Rotarians sitting together, dressed very casually, and seemingly staring at me in my newly pressed blue suit, crisp white shirt, and patterned tie.

"So what are you going to talk about, son?" asked an affable man in his 60s, assuming I was the speaker.

"Conquering the Fear of Public Speaking," I replied, with a slightly unnatural burst of enthusiasm.

"Oh, none of us have a problem with that, do we gentlemen?" he chuckled, and was joined by a chorus of loud laughter.

It's Do or Die

A little later, all six of them escorted me over to the meeting room and offered me a seat at a round table. They took the remaining six seats. After what seemed like a remarkably short business meeting, led by the affable gray-haired man, he began his introduction: "It's a pleasure to have with us today a young man who is not only speaking for free, but who's not trying to sell us anything." A spontaneous cheer went up in the room, and I could feel my heart pounding against my chest. "Please give a warm Rotary welcome to Mr. Steve Ozer."

With that, I walked up to the front of the room, stood there in my suit and tie, and told them the story of how I conquered the fear of public speaking. Even though the six of them stared at me like I was from Mars, my initial fear disappeared. As I was nearing the end of my talk, I became elated. I was overwhelmed by a sense of happiness and satisfaction, unlike anything I had ever felt before in my life.

I finished my speech, soaked up the applause, and then shook hands with each member of the audience. By now, I was feeling a calm, quiet sense of "mission accomplished" as I headed out of the restaurant and back to my car. I had finally done it—I had conquered the fear of public speaking forever.

The World Was My Oyster

At that point, I was determined to speak in front of any group that would have me. Since I didn't charge a fee, like many speakers just starting out, I found most everyone welcomed me. I spoke to Rotary Clubs, Lions Clubs, Kiwanis, Jaycees, and Optimists. I also spoke at senior centers, nursing homes, professional women's groups, and other community organizations. I spoke to anyone who would let me come in and talk about "Conquering the Fear of Public Speaking." Those presentations were instrumental in building my self-confidence as a public speaker. I still look back fondly at those experiences and the wonderful people I met.

After a year or so with Toastmasters, I had become friendly with a man there named Fred Fleitz. He owned a convenience store franchise where he worked during the day, and entertained audiences as a stand-up comic at night. One day, Fred offered me an interesting opportunity. He asked if I'd like to give a comedy routine at a charity fundraiser being sponsored by a local Lions Club. I would be one of eight stand-up comics who would perform at a nearby hotel.

Without thinking, I said yes. Then he told me there would be 500 people in the audience!

I remember that night at the fundraiser as if it were just yesterday. I stood in front of the crowd and confidently reeled off a 15-minute comedy routine. As I experienced wave after wave of laughter from the crowd, I couldn't help but think back to my high school talent show. Back then, I was sure that I would never have the courage to face 500 people and tell my own jokes. I felt I would always have to channel my creativity through someone else. Things have changed since then. Thank goodness.

Over the past 14 years, I have performed stand-up comedy in nightclubs, amphitheaters, banquets halls, and summer festivals. I've toured the circuit with a comedy troupe, the Sunday Comics, which helped raise more than $500,000 for charity. I've been hired to give speeches throughout the U.S. I've appeared on television many times and have been featured in scores of newspapers. In short, I've literally had the time of my life.

Remember this—if I can conquer the fear of public speaking, I'm 100 percent positive you can do it too. So stay with me…

True courage isn't shown by those who plow ahead and do something new without fear. It's demonstrated by those who are scared to death to do something new, but their dream is so strong that it drives them to do it anyway.

Chapter 3

The Fear of Being Different

DURING THE 20 YEARS I SPENT dodging my fears, I wasn't lacking for advice on how to conquer them. I talked with many people in the helping professions, as shared before. I read books, magazines, and newspapers. I recognized there were a lot of good ideas in what I was picking up. There was good advice about taking my mind off the fear before giving a presentation, about practicing what I was going to say before saying it, and about learning how to relax. I took it all in.

However, I must admit that something about all of this advice made me a little uneasy. It seemed to me that the doctors, psychologists, and other experts were unfailingly well-intentioned, and that their recommendations could certainly do a lot of good for a lot of people.

Nonetheless, there was definitely something missing. My instincts told me that even if I followed every recommendation to the letter, I would still freeze up at the mere thought of giving a presentation, let alone actually have the courage to go through with it.

What I came to realize is that I was seeking the truth about how to conquer the fear of public speaking, but only getting the half-truth. Half of it was useful; half of it was not. Half of it was realistic; half of it was not. Half of it was practical; half of it was not. The challenge was to figure out which was which.

Beginning with this chapter and each of the next four, we are going to examine the Four Half-Truths about Public Speaking:

Half-Truth #1—Imagining a Naked Audience Will Give
        You Self-Confidence
Half-Truth #2—It's No Big Deal. Just Do It!
Half-Truth #3—Relaxation Techniques Will Calm You
Half-Truth #4—If You Know Your Subject, You Won't
        Be Nervous

The first one, which we'll cover in this chapter, is my favorite:

Half-Truth #1—Imagining a Naked Audience Will Give You Self-Confidence

The idea here is to stride to the podium, face the audience, and use all of your powers of creative imagination to picture everyone wearing nothing more than a smile. You, of course, are fully dressed and in command. In your mind, the audience has been reduced to a shirtless, skirt-less, pants-less, hopeless mass of embarrassed humanity. You, however, demonstrate the confidence that comes from being the only one fully dressed in the formal (and drafty) auditorium. Look at these people. So ridiculous. So weak. So helpless. So…naked!

As you'll find with all of the half-truths, this advice is well-intentioned, and makes sense in a very fundamental way. The point here is to take your mind off of your own fears and project any feelings of inadequacy onto the audience, Face it, where would you rather be, cutting an imposing figure behind that podium or sitting buck naked just a few rows from your in-laws? By mentally taking the focus off of yourself, it can relieve the pressure and the fear of facing an audience. So at its core, Half-Truth #1 isn't half bad.

It's the other half; however, that's the challenge. This "naked" advice explicitly recommends that we mentally picture people sitting in the audience who are different than us; they're not wearing any clothes. My experience, as well as that of others, has shown that the fear of being different is one of the bedrock fears of those with public-speaking phobias. So if everyone is naked and we're not, it makes the situation even worse.

I suffered for a decade feeling helpless, worthless, ashamed, frightened, and alone in my fear of public speaking. As far as I knew, I was the only one in the world who had those feelings of shame. As far as I knew, I was the only one whose life had been disrupted in such a major way by it. And as far as I knew, I was the only one whose fear of public speaking consumed so much of my waking hours.

In my mind, I was different than everyone else. I was weaker, more helpless, less in control. This feeling of being different frightened me even more, because I longed to feel the same as everyone else. I wanted to feel as self-confident as the people appeared to be who I saw on television being interviewed every day. I wanted to feel as in control as the people appeared to be who ran the meetings I attended at my job with the chemical company. I wanted to feel as self-assured as the people seemed to be who introduced themselves to me at social gatherings.

In the end, it took me years to realize that the fear of being different is a major underlying factor in the fear of public speaking. Most of us sincerely want to fit in with the world around us—but, ironically, the fear gnawing at us within causes us to make ourselves feel helplessly different. Another part of the ironic truth is we need to be different from the average person to truly succeed, but we don't want to be a scared different.

A Cookie Is Just a Cookie

None of us starts out in life concerned about whether we are different or not; it's something many teach themselves out of fear of rejection. When our son, Alex, was two years old, we began looking for preschools in the area. My wife took him to visit a local school where a group of eight two-year-olds were happily playing with their toys under the supervision of a capable instructor.

At 3 o'clock, the instructor gathered together all the kids at a table for their midday snack, and invited Alex to join them. Alex eagerly grabbed the cookies and milk that he was offered, and began eating and drinking with gusto, kicking his legs happily under the table and smiling with delight. Little did he know that each of his eight peers were stopped mid-cookie. They were all staring at him with blank looks, wondering who this new kid was who was eating their cookies and acting like he'd been there for years.

Alex was at that wonderful age where he didn't care about what other kids thought of him. To him, a cookie was just a cookie. Unfortunately, for many of us, though, there comes a time when a cookie becomes more than a cookie—when we do care about what others think of us. Most people don't realize that, generally, it really needs to be none of our business what others think of us. It's all about them and their perceptions.

However, I've learned that many of those who are terrified of public speaking also are tremendously concerned about what people think. They want to be liked. They want to be respected. They want to be seen as having it all together. Most importantly, they don't want to be seen as different, i.e., weak, helpless, incompetent.

This fear of looking different often traces its roots to events early in life. For me, it goes back to the sixth grade.

As you'll recall, I became paralyzed with fear trying to deliver an oral book report. For others, the events are no less vivid and no less traumatic.

Vivid Recollections

There must be something about book reports. Janet, 33, an information technology coordinator for another chemical company, also traces her first terrifying experience to a similar experience in the sixth grade: "I was in grammar school, maybe 11 or 12 at the time, and I had to come up in front of the class, sit in a chair facing everyone, and give a book report," she recalls. "I was incredibly nervous, sweaty, and couldn't look at anyone. It felt like I couldn't breathe. I read through the report as fast as I could, ran back to my seat, and collapsed in my chair."

Amy, 36, an insurance company research analyst, remembers an incident in first grade when the teacher made everyone stand up and recite a tongue twister. Having the spotlight on her was disconcerting enough, she remembers, but having to recite a phrase that was designed to trip her up was even more humiliating. "I made an embarrassing flub," she recalls with a shudder, "and had to stand there while my classmates laughed at me." Amy remembers the scene vividly and says it had a painful and lasting impact on her ability to speak to groups later in life.

David, 34, a scientist, remembers a Spanish class in college where the professor used a particularly brutal exercise in off-the-cuff (spontaneous) speaking. The instructor would yell out a topic, and then point to a student at random to begin speaking in Spanish. To this day, David remembers the heartlessness of the teacher's approach. "It's hard enough to be put on the spot in English, let alone in a foreign language," he says, obviously affected with the painful memory.

Terry, 50, a telecommunications manager, has a vivid recollection of his "first time." "In college, I ran for class officer. As part of the campaign, I had to give a very short talk in the university chapel," he shares. "Well, about ten days before the talk was scheduled, I started thinking about it. Then I started worrying about it, and became terrified.

"On the day of the talk, I was a mess. I started taking medication to calm myself down. When I finally got up to make my presentation, I was practically incoherent, stumbling over words, and acting totally spaced out." Needless to say, Terry never became class officer; and, to this day, the incident remains a traumatic memory. This is certainly an example of what not to do.

Trigger Events

Janet, Amy, David, and Terry all recalled different circumstances when they first experienced their terror of public speaking. Janet was in grammar school; Amy faced a dozen six-year olds; David and Terry were in college. But even though these significant experiences were all different, nonetheless they all triggered the same sets of fears and emotions:

"What's Happening to Me?"

Each person describes his or her original experience as a jolt to the nervous system. The panic symptoms come on without warning, coursing through the body like an oncoming freight train, paralyzing the mind and immobilizing the body.

Often the only coherent thoughts that make it through these clanging alarm bells are, "What is happening to me?" "Why do I feel this way?" "What can I do to stop it?" and the most terrifying question of all, "Will I survive?" Feeling this way the first time can affect our attitude long-term in a very negative way, unless we do something about it. The world may seem darker, more unpredictable, and more ominous. We may see the world through the eyes of fear rather than those of hope and faith.

"I've Never Been So Humiliated!"

Being humiliated produces an awful feeling—the terrible sense that people are laughing at you on the inside. It causes an embarrassing flush of warmth and redness that's so obvious in our faces. Humiliation, whether it occurs for the first time at an early age or later in life, can rob us of our sense of security—a fundamental and unconscious belief that we can cope with anything life throws our way. For the first time, we may believe we "can't," and it's a truly frightening realization that can shake us to the core.

"When Will It Happen Again?"

The most overwhelming fear is that we will again experience the same sense of panic and desperation we had when we spoke in public for the first time. When that first, terrible, painful experience is finally over, when the clanging alarm bells have gone silent, when our body and mind are functioning normally again, another question slowly but surely creeps into our consciousness:

"When will it happen again?" This is the question that can come to haunt us. This is the question that plants the seed of avoidance in those of us who are terrified of public speaking. That seed can grow into a lifetime of exploding fears, career or business devastation, and personal despair—unless we conquer it.

The feelings brought on by those first terrifying incidents in life may instill in us the fear of being different, the fear that somehow we don't measure up to our classmates, our associates or colleagues, our friends, and even our families. That fear of being different can be a powerful motivator to hide our feelings of weakness, camouflage our fears, and show a different face to the world.

So We Put on Happy Faces

I described earlier how I presented an image of confidence, competence, and self-control, despite the fears that were eating me alive. I became an "Academy Award" winning actor. I mimicked the words and gestures of the self-confident, exuded self-esteem, and projected a can-do attitude that would make Dale Carnegie blush.

Eventually, much to my relief, I learned I wasn't unique. I wasn't the only one skilled at hiding fear and masquerading as someone else. In fact, I discovered that many people do it all the time.

Sally is a case in point. Her promotions through the ranks from administrative assistant to customer service manager were due not only to her competence and achievements, but to her positive, can-do attitude. "No one would ever know that I suffered from the fear of public speaking," she says. "I showed a tough exterior." Sally made her way through the corporation as an unflappable, unbeatable, unstoppable employee. When her boss had a challenge, he went to her. When employees had a concern, they went to her. She appeared to exude self-confidence, and it served her well—to a point.

Lurking underneath that confident exterior was a terrified little girl who froze during a solo performance in the high school choir. Sally never forgot the embarrassment and sense of humiliation that came from that episode, and she was determined never to show weakness in any form to anyone ever again. She did what many who fear public speaking do—she presented a completely different image to the world, one of supreme self-confidence.

George, a publisher in his mid-50s, is a sincere, likeable former engineer. In a period of time when his publishing business was taking a nosedive, he became a part of the networking industry. He was not only afraid of public speaking, but scared of people in general. His new business required that he make presentations to share his new business opportunity with prospective associates. His goal, which he accomplished, was to build an organization of independent business owners.

It only came out later, when he would speak to large groups as a leader that he used to be scared to death of people and public speaking. He had practiced and worked very hard to face and overcome his fear and became a dynamic and popular speaker.

Len, a 32-year-old freight auditor, believes that hiding his true feelings is a matter of self-preservation in his company. "When I worked with upper management, I needed to come across as someone who could stay cool under pressure, someone with an excellent sense of self-esteem," he says. "I couldn't afford to let my real fears come through."

Len's last comment is the most revealing: "I couldn't afford to let my real fears come through." Simply put, Len believed that showing any sign of weakness in the workplace was career suicide. Len didn't realize it, but he put his finger on one of the most emotionally and physically draining aspects of the fear of public speaking—the desperate and urgent need to keep these fears a secret.

A Deep, Dark Secret

I know that when I was knee-deep in the fear of public speaking, revealing the truth was like telling someone I had killed my mother and buried her in the basement. In my mind, that person would withdraw in horror, slowly backing away from me, glancing nervously from side to side in an attempt to escape this pitiful, miserable excuse of a human being. How could I be so weak? So incompetent? So utterly lacking in one of the most basic of human skills?

I was convinced that divulging my fear to the boss would spur secret meetings to decide on my replacement. My colleagues, filled with pity, would stare in disbelief at this hopeless, pathetic shell of a human being before them. My father and mother would scour their memories of my childhood for telltale clues as to where they went wrong. Even my dog would shake his head and walk away in disgust.

Frank, 59, a retired production supervisor, belongs in the Guinness Book of World Records for keeping it a secret. He managed to keep the fear of public speaking from his wife for 25 years. When he was scheduled to give a talk at work, he'd become physically ill the night before. His wife assumed he had the flu. At other times, he would toss and turn all night, his eyes wide open against the pillow. His wife felt so sorry for him and wished she could do something for the chronic insomnia that plagued him throughout the years. But still, she never knew what was really going on so she couldn't support him in getting the help he needed.

No Problem One-on-One

One of the greatest ironies of the fear of public speaking is that many of the same people who are terrified of speaking to groups of people are, in fact, excellent communicators in one-on-one situations. Jack, the counselor, is a perfect example. His warmth and sense of caring made him a superb counselor to adolescents. Even the most hardened juvenile delinquents responded to him positively in his individual therapy sessions with them. But as I shared, Jack was a nervous wreck in front of his fellow counselors, which was ultimately his undoing.

Mary, 39, a healthcare practitioner, is another example. "People have told me that I'm wonderful in one-on-one situations," she says. "I speak freely and openly, and I'm perceived as engaging, warm, and responsive." But she says things change dramatically when the audience increases from only one to two people. "I become gripped with fear, withdrawn, and closed," she says. No matter how good Mary is with individuals, she says that speaking in front of a group floods her with memories of a painful childhood.

"When I was young, my father told me I was stupid, I was ugly, that I wasn't good enough," she recalls painfully. "He made me believe that I didn't have anything of value to say to the world. The idea of standing before a group of people, gripped me with fear. Why would anyone dare to sit still for a stupid, ugly girl, with nothing useful to say to anybody?" Mary says she doesn't have those painful reminders when speaking with people one-on-one, which allows her natural, warm personality to come shining through. Later, we'll learn more about Mary and her success in conquering the fear of public speaking.

As we have discussed, the fear of being different is one of the common bonds that link all of these different people together. They fight a tremendous battle every day to hide their fears, show a brave face to the world, and fit in with all the other seemingly confident people. The final irony, however, is that the people who are so afraid of being different are, in fact, the same as nearly everyone else.

The Largest Minority

I've cited the cold, hard facts: Forty-one percent of Americans are more afraid of speaking before a group than of getting cancer. Okay, let's do the math: There are over 300 million people in the U.S. Forty-one percent of 300 million is 120 million. That means there are more than 100 million people in the U.S. alone, who are terrified of public speaking. Those of us who are in that group are in the largest minority group in the U.S.

No matter what country you live in, there is undoubtedly a large percentage of people afraid of speaking. The fear is so pervasive, that medical researchers have counted on it as an effective way to do research. In a study of heart patients at a hospital in New York, researchers developed a unique stress test. Patients, while hooked up to sophisticated stress-monitoring equipment, were required to give five-minute speeches about their personal flaws to a group of rather bored-looking hospital staff members in white lab coats. Not too surprisingly, about three quarters of the patients showed a slight increase in heart rates during the tests.

In another study, a group of medical residents was asked to make presentations to their superiors while hooked up to heart- monitoring equipment. During the presentations, all of their heart rates skyrocketed by more than 50 percent, while one frightened resident's heart rate went all the way up to 187, as if she were doing a heated aerobic workout.

The point of all this is that those who are terrified of public speaking are no different than anyone else. They're the same. All of the energy that goes into hiding the fear, covering up the pain, pretending to be someone else—is all wasted effort. It takes a lot of energy to hide this level of fear from your family, friends, associates, and colleagues.

It takes an enormous amount of stamina to avoid having to speak to groups year after year, decade after decade. And it's emotionally draining to think that we're weaker and less competent than almost everyone else in the world, not to mention the fact that it's simply untrue.

Hiding Is Wasted Energy

I have some great news for you. Reading this book makes you different than most people—in a positive way. You have taken the initiative to conquer the fear, a step most people never take. You have acknowledged that your life can be 1,000 percent better by conquering the fear. You understand what it can do for your life, your career or business, and your world in general.

It may still sound scary, and you may have some nagging doubts about whether you can do it, but you've taken the first step on the path to personal freedom. You are different in that respect. As you continue until you overcome your fear, like I did, you will reap the rewards that come from unleashing your potential.

True Courage

I used to sit in the audience and listen to people who were perfectly calm while speaking in public, and say to myself, "Now that's a brave person. Look at how they speak with ease in front of dozens of people. That's true courage."

I've come to understand over the years that true courage is not shown by the person who plows ahead and does something without fear. It's demonstrated by someone who is scared to death to do something, but who does it anyway. As Mark Twain said, "Courage is resistance to fear, mastery of fear—not absence of fear."

By reading this book, you have already demonstrated courage. You are starting to take action to conquer your fear. You are facing it and doing something about it. That's the kind of "different" we all need to be to move on in life, so we can accomplish our dreams and goals. Congratulations!

When you commit to breaking the cycle of avoidance, you'll take the single most important step in overcoming the fear of public speaking. You'll put yourself on an all-out effort to achieve what may seem to be your most impossible dream. By taking charge of your fear—and declaring that your life will no longer be run by it—you will see the stress and anxiety turn into positive, constructive, useful energy.

Chapter 4

The Fine Art of Avoidance

WE'VE EXPLORED THE FIRST half-truth and learned that naked people in the audience won't help you. People sitting in their birthday suits tend to make matters worse for the fearful public speaker, who is terrified of looking different. When push comes to shove, he or she would rather be buck naked and fitting in, than smartly attired and standing out. Half-Truth #2 is also well-intended and contains more than a little common sense.

Half-Truth #2—It's No Big Deal. Just Do It!

Public speaking? What's the big deal? No one will hurt you, right? Just get up and do it. Just stand up there, move your mouth up and down, let the words flow out, and do it. Simple.

Although you may want to disagree loudly, when people tell you public speaking is no big deal, they really are giving you only part of the truth. It's not an extreme sport. It doesn't threaten any of your extremities. You don't stand to lose any of your possessions, put your family in danger, or dangle your career or business by a thread. So what's the big deal?

The big deal, as we discussed earlier, is the fear of being different, which often stems from that first humiliating incident experienced early in life. I need to caution you, however, that not every humiliating experience, in your childhood or otherwise, is destined to be a traumatic experience.

For example, I remember the time I was only eight years old and decided to buy my mother a duck for her birthday. I was positive she would be overwhelmed with joy when I presented her with that quacking, waddling, web-footed, feathered creature I had bought from a kid down the block. I can still remember the day I took Mom out to the back yard to show her the gift. I waited for her tears of delight, only to be shattered when she gave me the look that said, "Did you save the receipt?"

Sure, I still wince when I think back to how awful and stupid I felt at the time, but it didn't create a fear of ducks or of giving gifts that haunted me the rest of my life. Still others can remember times early in life when they had very unpleasant experiences speaking in front of groups, much like the ones I described.

But they were still able to get back up there the next time and get the job done with a minimum of fear. So why is it that some people have humiliating experiences with public speaking and eventually develop debilitating fears, while others don't? The answer boils down to one word—avoidance.

The Addictive Nature of Avoidance

What I have learned is that people whose personal and professional or business lives have been disrupted by the fear of public speaking invariably have chosen to avoid it for long periods of time—years, often decades. That seed of avoidance is planted in certain early, humiliating episodes in life.

When you think about it, who in their right mind would want to repeat an experience marked by overwhelming anxiety, a furiously thumping heartbeat, near-paralyzed vocal cords, and close to a total shutdown of the central nervous system? It's no wonder that, when faced with the prospect of repeating those kinds of experiences, people choose avoidance over participation.

Avoidance can be like a powerful drug, faster acting and stronger than some stress relief medication and painkillers in reducing fear. Before, I described the many creative and destructive ways I used to avoid public speaking for nearly 20 years, and I can safely say that each time I avoided it, I felt remarkably better—at least temporarily.

As I've shared with you, my fears had grown to a point where someone even casually suggesting that I speak to a group would bring on the panic symptoms—profuse sweating, racing heartbeat, dizziness, and disorientation. But as soon as I found a way to avoid it—presto! The symptoms would subside immediately and dramatically. The sense of relief was powerful and overwhelming.

The challenge with the nature of avoidance is that it can become addictive. The first time you find a way to avoid public speaking, it feels good, very good. But from that first time, your dependence on avoidance grows stronger and stronger in order to return to that peaceful state of mind.

Finding new and seemingly clever ways to avoid public speaking can turn into a desperate web of disappointments, deceptions, and outright lies. This cannot only increase your challenges but decrease your integrity—truly a downward spiral.

The Side Effect of Guilt

Sally, the customer service manager, is a good example of the lengths someone will go in order to avoid public speaking. In every other respect, Sally exercises good judgment. She's dedicated, competent, and committed. But, as you'll recall, her good judgment went out the window when it came to public speaking.

When Sally's boss asked her to make a presentation to a group of customers on an important subject, she actively campaigned against the idea, arguing it was a terrible one. When her boss ended up canceling the session, Sally felt the "drug" of avoidance flood her system and provide immediate relief.

But it left a devastating side effect—guilt. She knew that she had not acted in the best interest of the company or its customers. She knew that she had let down her boss. But she did what she had been programmed to do from an early age—avoid public speaking.

Jeff, 41, CEO of an international trucking firm, is another one who has avoided public speaking for many years. But, instead of letting the boss down, he is the boss. Jeff incorrectly believed that even though he had avoided public speaking for a long time, the only one he had let down was himself.

"I know I need to be standing up in front of our employees regularly. I know it would help to focus our company, get it moving in new directions. But I just can't do it. I end up delegating presentations to one of my managers." So, although Jeff may not admit it, the whole truth is that he has and continues to let down a lot of people—not just himself—because of his avoidance. How about you?

John, the college student we talked about earlier, admitted as a 23-year-old university researcher, that he began honing his avoidance skills back in high school. "I learned how to make myself 'invisible' in class," he revealed. "I'd hide in the back and do everything I could not to be noticed. If I was called on, I'd pretend not to know the answer, even if I did."

In college, as you'll recall, John would avoid oral presentations in class, and if he couldn't avoid one, he'd drop the class immediately. In graduate school, John took the concept of avoidance to the next level. Whenever he had to make a presentation, he would recruit a friend to call up the professor with news of John's "illness." To this day, he still agonizes over every presentation and racks his brain for new and creative ways to avoid them.

Mary, the healthcare practitioner, is happy to be a part of the volunteer events she attends for women who have suffered abusive relationships. However, for years she has yearned to be in front of the group instead of behind the scenes. "I wanted to be up there talking to the group, but because of my fears, I always ended up behind the registration table or serving the meals," she says. "Even when it was my turn to be thanked at the end of the event, I would hide in the bathroom or in the kitchen. Friends would try to coax me out, but I wouldn't budge." Sound familiar?

The Negative Side of Avoidance

To this day, Sally, Jeff, John, and Mary continue to avoid public speaking and suffer the personal anguish and professional havoc that come from running away rather than embracing opportunities. However, fortunately, Mary fares better, as you'll see later on.

These people are caught in a vicious cycle—the avoidance-relief-avoidance cycle. Whenever they are asked to speak in front of a group, they suffer the agonizing symptoms that arise from their hidden fears. Then they do virtually anything they can think of to avoid speaking. When they're "avoidance-successful," the symptoms subside—until, that is, they get the next request to speak. Then the vicious cycle starts all over again.

The avoidance-relief-avoidance cycle definitely has an even darker side. Each episode of relief can actually reinforce the fear of public speaking, making it even stronger. As the months roll by, then the years, then the decades, the fear of public speaking can grow from feelings of general discomfort to full-blown, irrational terror. The fear can overtake any semblance of common sense, sometimes leading the terrified to take extraordinary actions to avoid his or her deepest fears.

Jack, the adolescent counselor, gave up the career he truly loved—social work—and became a mail carrier just to avoid his terrifying feelings. Today, instead of the deep sense of satisfaction he used to receive from helping young adults deal with their challenges, he works very hard sorting and delivering mail—which he doesn't enjoy. He comes home at the end of the day dead-tired, irritable, and in no mood to enjoy.

Although Jack feels the sense of relief that comes from the "drug" of avoidance, his relief is completely overwhelmed by the guilt over his actions. He hates his job and understandably feels he has let his family down. Over time, Jack has spiraled down the avoidance-relief-avoidance cycle, and now has hit rock bottom.

Fortunately, it is not necessary for you to hit rock bottom before you do something about conquering the fear of public speaking. Reading about how to do it is a great start, but you need to apply what you're learning. You can break the cycle of avoidance at any point along the way, and start the process of healing that will put you on the path to success. But first, there may be four things you are telling yourself that are preventing you from overcoming your fear. The following sections describe those four "self statements."

"I'm Just Too Afraid"

Of course you may feel this way. Just the idea of confronting what might be your deepest fear, let alone doing something about it, can be a terrifying one. But the fact that you are even reading this book and considering your options shows you have hope—even if it's just a glimmer. It shows you are at least willing to explore the idea of conquering your fear, and that is a tremendous first step. It also shows you believe the benefits of winning out over your fear might outweigh the challenge of getting there.

I can tell you from experience that being afraid of overcoming the fear of public speaking is perfectly natural, but unnecessary. When you follow "The Five Stages of Conquering the Fear of Public Speaking" covered later, you may be surprised at how little discomfort you'll feel as you go.

The way to overcome the fear is to do it in manageable increments, with what I call Brain Training, which we'll also cover a bit later. The idea is to reduce or eliminate the amount of discomfort at each stage so you are able to move on to each succeeding stage with confidence. If, at any point along the way, you feel very uncomfortable for any reason, you simply return to the activities in a previous stage to build your confidence.

The beauty of the process is that instead of feeling overwhelming discomfort as you move through the stages, you start to build confidence early on, and use this newfound confidence to pull you through each successive stage. It's probably hard to believe, but there may even come a point in the process where you (gulp) enjoy the challenge and look forward to speaking in front of the next group.

All along the way, instead of feeling overwhelming fear, you'll be tearing down the walls of fear that may have plagued you for years, decades, or even a lifetime. You can rid yourself of any sleepless nights you might have worrying about giving presentations. Wouldn't that be nice?

You can slow your racing heartbeat, calm your jitters, eliminate your quivering voice, stop your shaking knees, and give yourself a sense of peace when faced with the prospect of public speaking. Fortunately, the fear of public speaking is highly curable, and it's a whole lot easier than you may now think.

"It's Easier Not to Face Up to It"

On the surface, this makes sense. It may seem easier not to face up to your fears rather than to look them straight in the eye and do something about them. However, it depends upon what you mean by "easier." Is it easier to stay paralyzed by fear every time you're faced with making a presentation? Is it easier to search for new and creative ways to avoid speaking in public, even when it's hurting your career or business and your personal life? Is it easier to live your life with guilt, fear, and paranoia over something as benign as public speaking?

The truth is, most people who dread public speaking think life's a struggle. It takes them a tremendous amount of time, energy, and anxiety to deal with the fear. In the end, it makes life much harder than it has to be. If you're telling yourself that it's easier not to deal with it, you need to realize that you're dealing with it already. But it's likely you're doing it in a way that makes it extremely tough on yourself—the avoidance, the excuses, the secrets, the shame.

Take charge of your fears. Plant a stake in the ground and declare your life will no longer be run by them. Do this, and your stress and anxiety will turn into positive, constructive, useful energy which you can use to achieve your goals and realize your dreams. Sounds like a worthwhile reason to do it. Agree?

"I Can't Devote Years to Overcoming It"

At first blush, it would seem that any task as daunting as this would take years to accomplish. Turning back the clock on fears that may have started as far back as your early school years may seem like a formidable task. When I decided to conquer my fear back in 1987, I was certainly prepared to spend years doing it. Needless to say, I was surprised to see improvement in the first few weeks, and absolutely amazed and delighted to conquer it completely in only six months.

How long will it take you to overcome the fear? Because everyone is different, it may not happen in six months. Depending on the level of your fear, it could take more or even less time. But I have to say that I have seen even the most hardened cases of public speaking phobia cured in six months. It takes willingness. It takes commitment. It takes persistence. But it doesn't take years.

"I'll Never Be Any Good at It Anyway"

This is a particularly common mental block. The thinking goes, "Why do I need to invest any energy in this? Even if I become a calm public speaker, I won't be a good one." As rationalizations (telling yourself rational-sounding lies) go, this is an excellent one. It may be hard to picture yourself captivating a large crowd, bringing down the house with a particularly witty line.

Or you may find it hard to believe you can elicit tears of sympathy with a poignant story, when the most you may be able to do today is, perhaps, squeak out your name—without wetting yourself. But the fact is, there are some extraordinary public speakers waiting to be born who are trembling behind what might seem like insurmountable fears.

Gerry is one of them. He spent more than 15 years dodging and weaving the fear of public speaking all through his school and college years. Even with a college degree, he bounced from job to job with no real direction in life, secretly hiding his fear, and totally ashamed because he believed he could never pursue his real love—the law.

Gerry had wanted to be an attorney all his life, but believed he could never stand up in a court of law because of a terrible fear of public speaking. The idea of facing an opposing attorney, a jury of 12 strangers, a powerful judge, and a gallery of anxious spectators made his blood run cold. He didn't seem able to picture himself cool and confident, forcefully making the argument that would win his case. For years he told himself, like so many others do, that he would never be any good at it even if he had no fear of public speaking. So he didn't do anything about it.

Despite his reservations about his ability, Gerry finally made the decision that would change his life—he quit his job in Alabama and moved to Pennsylvania to take a ten-week course for people with public-speaking phobia. We happened to be in the same class and Gerry and I quickly became friends.

Over the next ten weeks, Gerry began to see in himself more than a glimmer of hope—he also began to see a glimmer of talent. Week after week, what slowly emerged was a personable young man with quick thinking and an easy smile. As the fear slowly loosened its grip on his mind and body, he began to engage the group more and more with his gentle wit and unexpected insight. The group began to look forward to his short talks, and it was easy to see by the teacher's smile that something special was going on here.

Gerry and I kept in touch for a while after the course ended and he moved back to Alabama. He continued to work on reducing his fears by joining Toastmasters. After several months in that group, he developed enough confidence to pursue a life-long dream—he applied for law school.

Many years went by before I heard about Gerry from another friend who was in the course. It turns out that Gerry had gone on to law school, and became the lawyer to beat in the mock trial contests held each year at the school. After graduating, he went on to establish himself as a successful trial lawyer in the southern U.S.

No matter what you may be telling yourself—I'm just too afraid; it'll take too long; or I'll never be any good at it—these are just ways to continue the cycle of avoidance that only reinforces your fear of public speaking. You can overcome it. Honestly, you can.

Later, you'll learn how to break the cycle of avoidance. You'll make a declaration to end the agony that comes from avoidance, the stress that comes from making excuses, and the anxiety that comes from suppressing your dreams and goals. You'll decide, once and for all, that you will do whatever it takes to conquer the fear of public speaking, and that you will persist until you do. It's worth it. It really is.

When you make that dramatic gesture, when you commit to breaking the cycle of avoidance, you will take the single most important step in this book. You'll put yourself on an all-out effort to achieve what may seem to be your most impossible dream—one that can help you go to the top.

One of the keys to overcoming the fear of public speaking is to let go of the fear of the symptoms—to stop attaching significance to them. Those symptoms are just natural human responses to uncomfortable situations.

Chapter 5

The Challenge of the Symptoms

HALF-TRUTH #3 IS ANOTHER piece of wisdom with a split personality. It may be a part of the solution but, especially for those with long-term, deeply entrenched fear, more help is needed.

Half-Truth #3—Relaxation Techniques Will Do the Trick

Half of the truth is that relaxation techniques can be an effective way to soothe you, whether you're talking to your local garden club, doing a training session for your colleagues or associates, or addressing a large convention. These time-tested techniques for regulating your breathing, slowing your heart rate, and sharpening your mind are a critical part of the fear-fighting arsenal.

The other half of the half-truth is that relaxation techniques are totally ineffective for the person who has avoided public speaking for years. That's because, as we learned in the previous chapter, the symptoms tend to turbo-charge themselves through years of avoidance. It's the fear of the symptoms that can drive people like you and me to avoid public speaking for years on end.

What's Happening to Me?

Julie, 34, a sales manager for a home healthcare firm, remembers what it felt like to give her first speech as a dietician a number of years ago: "I had no idea that the symptoms were coming on," she vividly recalls. "All of a sudden, I felt a pounding in my head, and my voice sounded like an echo to me. Then, my voice started to crack, and my mouth went totally dry. To this day, I don't remember what I said; all I remember was finishing up the presentation as fast as I could. I was terribly embarrassed."

Janet, the information technology coordinator, remembers what it was like to assist the pastor with readings in church when she was in her 20s. "My heart would pound uncontrollably," she shares. "I could barely talk; I'd be gasping for air. And my leg would shake visibly. Even after I sat down, I'd still be shaking."

Jeff, the trucking company CEO, noticed a pattern of symptoms that began in the tenth grade. "No matter how organized or prepared I was, I would start getting nervous, and then I'd start losing focus. I'd begin to perspire heavily. My face would turn bright red. I'd begin stuttering, tripping over words, and find it hard to recover."

Julie, Janet, and Jeff know what it's like to experience the challenge of the symptoms. They catch you off guard. They negatively affect various parts of your body, causing you to feel defenseless and out of control. You may believe you're losing control over your mind and body, and it can be truly scary—something you are certain to remember.

Here are 11 typical symptoms that can occur in those who fear public speaking:

1. Quavering Voice
2. Pounding Heart
3. Red Face
4. Shaky Hands
5. Sweaty Palms
6. Dribbling Armpit
7. Shaky Knees
8. Cotton Mouth
9. Nauseous Stomach

10. Dizzy Head
11. Mind Block

It's true that experiencing these symptoms is certainly uncomfortable. However, be reassured that as you work to conquer your fear, the symptoms dissipate and could even disappear. Also be encouraged that, in most cases, the audience is not aware of how you're feeling. What seems so obvious to you is rarely so to the audience.

Since we're all different, not everyone experiences each of them or in the same combinations, and the degree of intensity may vary. But I'm sure you will recognize one or more of them.

1. The Quavering Voice

No matter how intent you are in sounding confident to your audience, nothing can destroy that confidence faster than hearing your own voice buckling under pressure. You may want to sound like the voice of authority booming out over the loud- speakers, immediately hushing the audience to rapt silence. But instead, what you may hear is a thin, weak, mousy, shaking, quivering, quavering, squeak of a voice.

No matter what the audience is actually hearing, you are probably very disappointed that your voice has given away any lack of confidence you may be feeling. (I used to feel like a weak, ineffectual, hopeless, helpless excuse for a human being.) You may be sure that everyone in the audience is shaking their heads and muttering to themselves, "What are you doing up there, with that cricket-like chirp of a voice? I expected the voice of authority; the voice of experience; the voice of confidence. Not some unintelligible, finch-like babble!" The truth is they may not even notice.

2. The Pounding Heart

This can be a real challenge. The pounding heart seems to come out of nowhere and overtakes your body like a run-away freight train. You can't ignore this little organ as it relentlessly pounds thump, thump, thump, inside your chest. It may feel like you're having a heart attack—like you're seconds away from collapsing.

Of course, the possibility that you might pass out in front of an audience is about the worst thing you may believe could potentially happen. You might think the pain and embarrassment would be too hard to bear.

That's what makes the pounding heartbeat one of the most challenging symptoms of all. You may tell yourself you're losing it, you're out of control, and you might not even make it through the presentation alive. If there is one universal symptom, this is it.

3. The Red Face

Not everyone gets a red face when they stand in front of a group, but those who do tend to see it as Armageddon. They see it as a personal meltdown, a flaring, glaring, livid reminder to the audience of the helpless person before them. It's as if the audience sees the red face as representing all of the shame, embarrassment, and feelings of incompetence wrapped up in one glowing ember, standing out like a red flare on the highway at night.

Those who get flushed if they get nervous are sure that members of the audience are elbowing their companions, saying, "Look at that taillight up there (snicker, snicker). His head is lit up like a jack-o-lantern at Halloween. He could hire himself out as a red traffic light! Where'd he get that sunburn?" Of course, no matter what the audience is really observing or thinking, the speaker is absolutely positive they're seeing red.

4. The Shaky Hands

This is my personal favorite. What could shout out "Nervous speaker!" more than a pair of quaking, shaking hands? No matter how confident your voice sounds, no matter how much you keep that thumping heart under control, you're probably sure those rattling limb extensions are telegraphing your audience that you have nerves of Jello®.

I've struggled with this symptom for years, even after conquering the fear of public speaking. It seems no matter how confident or well-prepared I am, my shaking hands still make me feel a little weak and helpless, despite the fact the audience doesn't really notice. It's really no big deal though.

To this day, I won't use a laser pointer, because that fine, little red dot on the screen tends to shake around a lot, even with a relatively steady hand. In my heart of hearts, I know that shaky hands don't mean a thing when it comes to public speaking. Nevertheless, I rarely pick up a sheet of paper I'm reading to an audience for fear they'll notice my quivering extensions. This is just an idiosyncrasy of mine and you may not have this challenge at all.

5. The Sweaty Palms

The slick beads of moisture accumulating on the palms are as welcome as a thunderstorm at an outside wedding. Although this is one symptom that is truly private, it still used to feed into my perception that my body functions were failing. At one time, I had sweaty palms, but no more.

6. The Dribbling Armpit

A mostly private symptom is the dribbling armpit. That is where a single drop of sweat forms under one of your arms, grows in size, then becomes a secret rivulet, making its way down your side, your leg, to the waiting puddle on the floor. (Maybe yours don't make it all the way to the floor.)

Another situation with armpit sweat is that for some, especially men, it can be so intense that it soaks that entire area of their shirts. It can be hidden by wearing a suit coat.

7. The Shaky Knees

If I had my choice between shaky hands and shaky knees, I'd probably choose shaky knees. But that's because I don't wear a skirt and can hide behind a podium if I choose. Many people with public-speaking phobia believe the shaky knees are a visible sign of profound weakness.

I have known more than one beginning public speaker who has chosen to give presentations while sitting, to avoid giving away their secret of the shaky knees. This symptom can be as challenging as any other because it carries with it the unpleasant and extremely unlikely possibility that the two appendages holding you up might buckle at any minute.

People with shaky knees tend to think the audience is focused on their quivering kneecaps, just waiting for their bodies to buckle, fold, and drop to the stage. Fortunately, this is just their nervous projection rather than reality.

You've probably heard of the industrial strength version of the shaky knees, called knocking knees. Although I have never experienced this myself, nor seen it happen to anyone else, acute anxiety can, supposedly, cause kneecaps to knock together rapidly, making a woodpecker-like sound. Personally, I think someone's pulling my leg (just kidding).

8. The Cotton Mouth

Did you ever wonder why most professional public speakers have a glass of water close by? It's because they know what it's like to speak with the cottonmouth. For some people, nervousness tends to dry out the mouth, turning it into an arid, barren, desert wasteland. All traces of saliva disappear and the mouth feels like it's filled with six or seven wads of cotton. Trying to talk with a mouth stuffed like that may be fun in your spare time; but it's exasperating when you're endeavoring to make a point in front of a hundred members of your company or organization.

I was attacked by the cottonmouth once when speaking to a group of attorneys and did not have a glass of water close by. What was really scary was that, after a while, the only sounds I could pronounce with authority were vowels. Soon, my lips began sticking together, making it very difficult to pronounce any words that didn't start with the letter "b." I quickly realized that if someone didn't bring me a glass of water soon, my speech would be reduced to a series of sheep-like, baa-baa-baa sounds! Since then, I've never given a presentation without a glass of water more than 12 inches away.

Like most symptoms, however, the cotton mouth isn't noticeable to the audience unless it gets really bad, like in the example above. But for someone who is terrified of public speaking, it's another sign of weakness—a sign that the body's automatic reflexes have taken control.

9. The Nauseous Stomach

This one really used to make me sick. There are more than a few people who become physically nauseous at the prospect of public speaking. The nauseous stomach can be an unpredictable symptom.

I'll never forget a fellow student, Jake, who was in my public-speaking phobia class. Jake was different from everyone else in the class in that he hadn't avoided public speaking all his life. In fact, in his position as a mechanical engineer, part of his job was to make presentations every week. Jake told us that he threw up before every talk. His nausea had plagued him for years and would not subside no matter how regularly he spoke.

Jake told the class about an unusual series of events that had recently taken place in his life. He had gone to see his doctor for the follow-up to a routine physical exam, where he received some devastating news. He was suffering from a terminal disease, and the doctor had given him only six months to live. The news hit him like a sucker-punch to the stomach—he would be dead in less than a year.

Physically, Jake still felt fine, despite the fact he was reeling emotionally. To keep his mind off of his challenges, Jake decided to keep going to work. But when he returned the next week, sure enough, he was required to give another presentation.

That's when something truly strange happened. Ten minutes before the presentation, when he'd usually be getting sick in the bathroom, Jake felt absolutely fine. No nausea. No panic. No restlessness. In fact, he had no qualms whatsoever about getting up in front of the group. That week he was completely at ease with his presentation, sailing through it without so much as a thumping heart or a sweaty brow.

What was going on here? Jake told us that he had finally put the fear of public speaking in perspective: "Why should I be afraid to speak when I was going to die, for crying out loud? For the first time in my life, I knew what fear was all about, and it wasn't about facing a group of people. It was about wasting away from a terrifying 'disease'!"

From that point on, Jake was cured of the nauseous stomach. In fact, he was cured of the fear of public speaking. For Jake, it was the best of times and the worst of times.

And it lasted only two weeks. His doctor had called him in to discuss the latest lab report, and from the look on the doctor's face, Jake knew something was wrong. It turned out there had been a serious mistake. Jake was diagnosed incorrectly—he was not dying of a terminal disease. He was fine. Ecstatic, Jake rushed home to break the wonderful news to his family. The next day, he went back to work and, sure enough, they asked him to make a presentation.

Ten minutes before the presentation, Jake felt the familiar rumblings in his stomach, and ran down the hall to the bathroom. The fear of public speaking again had reared its ugly head and things were back in perspective. Public speaking was the scariest thing in the world—once again.

10. The Dizzy Head

The dizzy head can make you feel like you're about to pass out. It's that unmistakable woozy feeling, like the world is just a little off balance, and you're about to tip over. When you look out over the audience, everything's just a bit blurred, and the ceiling lines don't seem exactly perpendicular to the lines of the wall.

The dizzy head is a challenging symptom because it makes you feel that you're about to lose complete mental control. Fortunately you don't, of course, unless you progress to the eleventh and final symptom of the fear of public speaking...

11. The Mind Block

I saved the best for last. The mind block is the one symptom audiences can truly notice—the mind simply goes blank. Zap. Zero. Nada. Nothing. The brain, which just a moment ago had been filled with great intentions, moving words, invaluable insights, seemingly be- comes wiped clean in the blink of an eye.

If you've ever seen someone who begins faltering, stuttering, hesitating, and pausing for what seems an inordinate amount of time, chances are they are suffering from the mind block. Is it any wonder the mind goes blank when the rest of the body may be experiencing one or more of the other symptoms?

Only someone with superhuman endurance could think straight if his or her body is being consumed by the pounding heart, the quavering voice, the shaky hands, and the dizzy head, or any of the other symptoms. It's an almost impossible task.

I still suffer from mind block occasionally. I remember doing a comedy routine in front of 500 people at a singles night for a charity fundraiser a few years back. Despite having successfully used the material many times, I bombed. At first, I thought I could hear crickets in the back of the room as I delivered the punch lines. Then the "noise level in the room" began to rise, and finally, I was drowned out by the "dull roar" in the room. Then my mind blanked out.

As luck would have it, my show was being taped for local cable television, and I had the unfortunate experience of watching it a week later. It wasn't until then that I realized I had accidentally skipped entire chunks of my routine. The mind block was out and in full force. But I survived it and now I can laugh about it.

If you're like me, you've experienced one or more of the eleven symptoms, and you know what it feels like to have your body sound the alarm bells. It's a challenging experience, made all the more challenging because many of us tend to attach great significance to these symptoms.

A pounding heart might not be just a pounding heart. It may seem to you to be a physical manifestation of the helplessness you feel in doing what appears to come so easily to other people. A red face might not just be a red face.

It might seem like a public and visible confession that you are not worthy of speaking before others. And a shaky hand may not be just a shaky hand. It might seem like a declaration to the audience that you have more than just private jitters—that you are standing on very shaky ground indeed.

The Invisible Symptoms

As I mentioned earlier, these symptoms are practically invisible to the audience. As much as they may fill us with fear and shame, amazingly, others usually can't tell. That's because, in our own minds, we might be dramatically inflating the impact and noticeability of those symptoms.

For example, we may be sure that a pounding heart can be seen through our clothing—a rippling blouse, a wavering lapel—when that's just not true. We might be sure people can see our hands and knees shaking, when, actually, it is usually impossible to see them—even from the front row. We may be certain that someone sees the color of our face as an embarrassing, glowing ember, instead of the warm and natural blush it probably appears to be.

Earlier, I described how our public-speaking phobia group used videotape to get a more objective view of how our symptoms actually appeared to an audience. The difference between how my classmates felt and how they looked was dramatic.

There was one poor woman who I'll always remember. When it was her first time to speak in front of the group, she had to be literally carried, one man under each arm, to the front of the room. With the camera rolling, she valiantly delivered her presentation, battling what must have been all of the eleven symptoms of the fear of public speaking.

Watching the videotape of her presentation was a turning point for me. She looked good. She sounded good. And she didn't even look nervous.

That's when it dawned on me how invisible most of these symptoms actually are to others, and why it is such a waste of energy to worry about how we look and sound when speaking in front of people. We probably tend to blow them out of proportion—assuming the audience notices everything. Just because we are acutely aware of these symptoms simply doesn't mean the audience is. Remember that.

You May Need to Let Go

Regardless of how we look to others, one of the keys to overcoming the fear of public speaking is to let go of the fear of the symptoms—to stop attaching significance to them. A pounding heart is a pounding heart, nothing more. A red face is a red face, that's all. And a quavering voice is a quavering voice. Tell yourself you'll blast through them. All of these symptoms are just natural human responses to uncomfortable situations.

As you proceed through the Five Stages of Conquering the Fear of Public Speaking in Part II, you'll begin seeing these symptoms subside. As they do, you will start thinking less and less of them as obstacles to speaking in front of groups.

As the symptoms dissipate, keep in mind, as I noted before, they may never disappear entirely. But you'll find that's okay. Even today, whenever I'm introduced to speak my heart beats faster than normal, not slowing down until after I launch into my presentation. But when I feel my heart pounding for those few seconds, there's one big difference from the way I used to feel—I don't care. It doesn't mean anything to me anymore.

My new attitude is that those extra heartbeats are pumping me full of extra energy that will translate into a more exciting, dynamic presentation. My heart is literally pumping me up. Beware of the public speaker who claims he or she never gets nervous before a presentation—they are probably as dull as an egg timer!

Letting go of the fear of the symptoms is a key part of overcoming your reluctance to speak. When you do, you will gain a sense of power and freedom that cannot be described. You'll love it.

Seeing your mistakes as perfectly human goes a long way toward finding peace of mind.

Chapter 6

The Things You May Be Telling Yourself

YEARS AGO, WHEN my nervous system would do somersaults at the mere thought of public speaking, I was plagued with a nagging question—Why? Why was my pulse racing? Why were my knees weak? Why was my stomach doing flip-flops? And why was it all happening automatically, instantaneously, and without warning?

It was like being backed into a corner by someone who was about to take my life. My body would cry out, looking for a way to escape, to run and hide from a situation that spelled imminent physical danger.

Fight or Flight

Part of the answer lies in the fight-or-flight response, which can be traced back to our primitive ancestors. Early man, when faced with a life-threatening situation, would experience a complex series of psychological and physiological responses that would prepare him to either fight the battle or escape from the threat.

The threatening image, transmitted from one or more of the senses to the brain, would set off internal "alarm bells," preparing the body for the physical challenge of fighting or running. These alarm bells included a racing heartbeat, shallow breathing, pro- fuse sweating, heightened senses, and an overwhelming desire to either fight to the death or run for your life.

Experts believe this fight-or-flight response became part of mankind's genetic code long after it was needed for daily survival. Anyone who has suffered from a phobia—whether it be fear of flying, enclosed spaces, heights, or something else—has experienced the fight-or-flight response in one way or another. For these people, the "life-threatening" image could be an airplane, an elevator, a tall building...or an audience.

For those who suffer from fear of public speaking, the fight-or-flight response can be triggered by the image of an expectant crowd, a solitary podium on a bare stage, a microphone in hand, or something else representing that experience. Regardless of the image that triggers it, the body's response is dramatic—a pounding heart, rapid breathing, and profuse sweating that sends a clear message: fight or run.

Are You Telling Yourself Speaking Is More Than Unpleasant?

The fight-or-flight response is only a part of the answer to the question: Why do some people's bodies react so violently to the thought of public speaking when it is clearly not a life-threatening situation? The other part lies with what you may be telling yourself. It is the conscious and unconscious whisperings in your own ear that can be the catalyst to turn the benign image of an expectant audience into the perception of a serious threat.

Those of us who dread public speaking inadvertently sound the alarm bells by signaling to our central nervous systems that there is more at stake here than simply talking to other people. Consciously and unconsciously, we may be raising the stakes on our performance by attaching extra meaning to something we literally do every day—talk to people. In the recesses of our subconscious, we may be convincing ourselves that speaking to a group is more than unpleasant—it spells imminent personal and professional disaster, which brings us to...

Half-Truth #4—If You Know Your Subject You Won't Be Nervous

As in all the half-truths, there is quite a bit of wisdom in this. For many people, being knowledgeable about a subject is the key to confidence. They stand before a group, secure in their knowledge of the topic, and prepared to share it with a receptive audience. This helps them control the "butterflies" that naturally accompany almost any presentation, at least at the beginning. In their minds, the worst thing that could happen is that the audience will lose interest before the presentation is over. They don't let this stop them.

For many of us, however, the whole truth is not as pretty. It doesn't matter whether we know the subject matter inside and out, if we are considered experts in our fields, and if we've accumulated knowledge over a period of years or even decades. What does matter is if we've silently told ourselves, perhaps for much if not most of our lives, that public speaking is a life-threatening situation that we need to avoid at all costs.

Jeff, the CEO of the transportation company, is a case in point. At 40, he is at a stage in life where he could justifiably feel comfortable in sharing his trucking industry knowledge with his peers. From his perch, he oversees the logistics of a fleet of 300 rigs that deliver goods throughout the U.S., Canada, and Mexico. Despite his professional accomplishments, Jeff still believes his fear of public speaking has held him back both professionally and personally.

"I can remember being asked to perform in a school play in the seventh grade, and even though I had only four or five lines, I was extremely nervous," he says. "I could barely spit them out." At 12, Jeff recalls, he began associating anxiety with the act of speaking in front of people. In the back of his mind, he began telling himself that public speaking was a dangerous activity—one that brought on terrifying and inexplicable symptoms. For him, the fact that his heart would beat out of control, his face would flush bright red, and his mind would go blank, were clear signs that he needed to avoid public speaking at all costs.

"As I got older, I thought that knowing my subject and being well organized would help me deal with the fear, but it didn't," he says. "I can't tell you how many opportunities I lost to grow professionally because of it." When asked to make a presentation at a national transportation conference, he agonized over the decision, but finally said no.

"Here I was offered a golden opportunity to speak on a national platform about our company's success in Mexico," he shares. "But instead of jumping at the chance, I turned it down because of my fear of public speaking. I still kick myself for being so foolish, so weak."

Jeff even avoids speaking to large groups of employees at his own company. "I know I need to get up there and talk to them about what's going well and what isn't," he says. "But, instead, I rely on other managers to do it for me. I'm losing the opportunity to get out important messages, but, in the back of my mind, I know it would be disastrous.

I would be unfocused, I'd lose my train of thought, and I'd feel miserable. Sure, if I was able to speak to all of our employees at once, I know I'd be more successful in moving this company in a new direction. But I just can't do it."

Jeff is embarrassed to admit that his fear of public speaking even extends to his family life. "I have three beautiful children, and I'd love to be able to entertain them and their friends by telling stories. It would be fulfilling for me, and it would be a great way to get them away from the television. But I can't do it. The fear is there, and I hate to think what I would look like if I went to tell a story and lost my train of thought or became flushed. It would be painful and embarrassing."

Len, 48, a manager with a large telecommunications firm, is an- other one who discovered that knowing his subject was anything but the key to tranquility. "I'll never forget the time when I was asked to teach organizational behavior concepts to a large group of employees at my company," he says. "These were foreign concepts to most people, and in the back of my mind I was sure I'd be speaking to a hostile audience."

Despite Len's expertise and credibility in the subject matter, he began to doubt his own ability. "I began asking myself, 'Am I qualified to teach this course? Is this topic really relevant? Is this worth people's time?' "

In the end, Len was so unsure of himself, so terrified of looking stupid, that his symptoms got the best of him. "My stomach was tied in knots," he remembers painfully. "I was unfocused. I reacted defensively to some of the questions. At the end of the presentation, I felt like crying."

Len believes he undermined his own performance—by the things he told himself. Quite consciously, he set himself up for failure by telling himself he was unworthy of standing before the group. He questioned his own qualifications, and convinced himself the audience would be hostile and unreceptive. He was sure no one wanted to be there.

With that frame of mind, it was no surprise that his body reacted the way it did. Faced by what he was convinced was a threatening situation (fight-or-flight) and fed by his own self- defeating thoughts, the outcome of his presentation became a self- fulfilling prophecy. In his mind he had failed, and that translated into his real-life experience.

The "High Wire Act"

Julie Weiss is the psychologist I mentioned earlier who treats people with public-speaking phobia at her practice in

Philadelphia, PA. She believes there are good reasons why many people see public speaking as a high-risk activity.

"Speaking in front of a group is a high-wire act for many people," she explains. "It's a unique form of communication in which there is high visibility, high exposure, with very little feedback and support from the listeners. To be a confident public speaker, it's important to learn how to quiet the inner critic and instead say supportive things to yourself." She likens it to a cartoon character who runs off a cliff and stays suspended in midair until he realizes there is nothing holding him up.

"When we stand in front of an audience, we come face to face with our inner worlds," she explains. "With no feedback from the audience and no visible means of support, we are left with our own thoughts. And what we silently tell ourselves is based on our own thoughts, beliefs, and experiences. Those who are comfortable with public speaking silently reinforce themselves, creating a sense of accomplishment they will feel as a result of a successful presentation."

"For those who are terrified of public speaking, however, the thoughts are often negative, highly critical, and self-defeating," she says. "Sometimes they are a replay of feelings that have been internalized since childhood.

"If someone was raised by parents who were constantly harsh and critical," she shares, "those harsh judgments will often resurface unconsciously when that person speaks in front of a group. Internally, they'll focus on their supposed flaws, their incompetence, their stupidity, their worthlessness—all of the things they came to believe about themselves when they were growing up."

Dr. Weiss gives another example where a child is raised in a household where the parents are always on the verge of divorce. "Growing up in a household like that can make a child feel like anything he or she does wrong may precipitate the divorce. Later in life, that person may grow to attach tremendous significance to the act of public speaking, and feel that giving anything but a perfect performance will spell disaster."

So, what goes through the mind of someone who attaches great meaning to the act of public speaking, and attempts the high-wire act? Dr. Weiss gives three examples of scary "what-if" thoughts we may tell ourselves:

1. "I'm really terrible at this." It's easy to see why someone who is terrified of public speaking would whisper this to them- selves, consciously or unconsciously. Panicked speakers are often harshly critical of themselves, far more than a typical member of the audience would be on them.

When standing in front of an audience they feel emotionally exposed, vulnerable, open to criticism. They are flooded with feelings of insecurity, worthlessness, helplessness, and shame. The physiological symptoms only confirm their worst fears. The quavering voice, flushed face, and wobbly knees take on much greater significance than simple nervousness. They become outward signs of their feelings of weakness, incompetence, and stupidity.

2. "This speech is do or die." Because people with the public- speaking phobia attach great meaning to the moment, they convince themselves that a single presentation will have dramatic consequences on their careers or businesses, their public standing, or even their social lives. They believe that anything less than a perfect presentation will subject themselves to extreme disgrace and humiliation.

Because the stakes are so high, any perceived imperfection is magnified a thousand fold in their minds. A quavering voice is seen as a disastrous sign of incompetence; a momentary lapse in thought is seen as a complete breakdown; a red face and shaking hands confirm their feelings of weakness, helplessness, and shame.

3. "If I'm not perfect, no one will love me." Dr. Weiss explains that people who grew up in a household where they experienced unconditional love often feel more secure in public speaking. Unconditional love means that love is provided with no requirements. If children feel their parents will only love them if they are intelligent, successful in school, or highly gifted, they don't experience unconditional love.

"People who confuse love and approval tend to have more anxiety in a public-speaking setting," says Dr. Weiss, "because they tend to base their self-esteem on how they perform."

So, if you grew up in a household where love had its conditions, is there hope for you as a public speaker? "Absolutely," explains Dr. Weiss, "Unconditional love is not something only our parents [or others] can bestow on us, but something we can give ourselves," she says. "The presence of unconditional love in your life, even from yourself, can greatly reduce anxiety. That way, a speech is just a speech, rather than a measure of who you are.

Unconditional love is about forgiveness—forgiveness of our imperfections, forgiveness of our faults, forgiveness of the impossibly high expectations we place on ourselves," Dr. Weiss explains. "When people talk about love and forgiveness, they are usually talking about other people. But loving yourself unconditionally and forgiving yourself completely can build a foundation for confidence in public speaking." Know that you are now okay and that you always have been okay.

Later we'll talk about how to recognize and prepare for the negative things you may be telling yourself that can sabotage a presentation. You'll learn how to redirect those self- communications into positive energy. Those techniques can be even more powerful when we develop what Dr. Weiss calls "trusting bonds" with ourselves. "It is possible to develop a loving acceptance of yourself, even if you didn't experience that kind of love when growing up," she says. She recommends that we strive for three areas of forgiveness and acceptance:

1. Learn to forgive your own flaws. Dr. Weiss points out that history has yet to provide the perfect human being, yet perfection is still what many of us strive for. Certainly we would all love to be supremely happy all the time, universally respected, and unequivocally successful. But the fact is, all of us fall short of these ideals for one perfectly acceptable reason—we're human.

The person who forgives him or herself for being human and making mistakes, stands a much better chance of becoming a comfortable public speaker than one who sees each flaw as a personal catastrophe. Recognizing, accepting, and even loving our own flawed humanity is a priceless gift we can give ourselves.

2. Celebrate your uniqueness. Whether it is your sense of humor, your compassion, your tenacity, your sense of adventure, your creativity, a combination of these and other qualities, or something else, recognize what it is that makes you special. Make that an unshakable foundation of your self-worth. Centering yourself around a core set of unique qualities will help to gird you against the inevitable disappointments of life, and constantly remind you of the value you bring to others' lives.

3. Look at your mistakes with compassion and understanding. Seeing your mistakes as perfectly human goes a long way toward finding peace of mind. People who are terrified of public speaking can be notoriously judgmental of their own mistakes and harshly critical of their perceived shortcomings. Conversely, people who are comfortable at public speaking take their mistakes in stride. They realize they may make them. When they do, they recognize them for what they are (learning experiences), learn from them, and move on.

*S*how your brain that standing in front of a group is not painful—that transmitting the fight-or-flight response is an inappropriate reaction to a speaking situation. Speak because you have something valuable to share with the audience. It's not about you—it's about them. Put speaking into the proper perspective.

Chapter 7

The Power of Brain Training— Show Your Brain Who's Boss!

AS WE DISCUSSED, THE THINGS you may be telling yourself can undermine your sense of worth and of having self-control. Those of us who are terrified of public speaking know that losing control is about the worst thing that can happen. In our minds, we may see losing control of our body's reactions as a precursor to losing control of everything else—our professions or businesses, our families, our friends, and the like.

Public Speaking Is a Drug-Free Zone

This book is about finding the strength within yourself to conquer the fear, once and for all, without the need to depend on anything external to see you through. It's about learning to replace the fear and anxiety with a sense of enjoyment and positive anticipation at the prospect of public speaking. It's about learning to feel good about public speaking—having a positive mental outlook and an other-centered focus that will obliterate the fear. Remember, take your eyes off yourself and focus on sharing what you have to offer. This helps nervousness melt away.

Brain Training—Not Brainwashing

So, what's the answer? I call it Brain Training—a way to train your brain to respond differently to the prospect of public speaking. Show your brain that standing in front of a group is not a painful experience—that instantly transmitting the fight-or-flight response is an inappropriate reaction to a speaking situation.

Speak because you have something valuable to share with the audience. It's not about you—it's about them. In short, put things in the proper perspective. Show your brain who's boss!

Brain Training is not brainwashing. It is simply a powerful, natural way to conquer the fear of public speaking by using your head.

I used to believe that when it came to Brain Training, you had to leave it to professionals, namely psychiatrists and psychologists. They are the ones schooled and licensed to probe the underpinnings of personal fears. I visited more than one who put me on the couch to psychoanalyze the roots of my fear of public speaking.

To their great dismay, they found I had no toxic parents, no childhood trauma, no dramatic upheaval. Bad toilet training? No. Physical or verbal abuse? None. Crushing personal disappointment? Nope. Often, the couch would feel so comfortable, I'd do everything I could to keep from dozing off, then look over to find the psychologist snoozing peacefully.

Training your brain boils down to two things: thinking and doing things differently. By thinking about some things differently and by doing some things differently, you can dramatically change the way your brain reacts to the prospect of public speaking.

Changing What You Think and Do

Since the brain is not an empty vessel, you have been brain-training for many years. You have been thinking certain things about public speaking, probably from an early age, and most likely talking to yourself negatively about it for many years—consciously or unconsciously. If you could listen in on the conversation, it might sound something like this:

"There's nothing that terrifies me more than having to speak in front of a group of people. If I had to do it, I'd just die. I know that my entire body would be overtaken by horrible symptoms, and I'd probably collapse in front of the audience. I can't take that chance. My career (or business) and reputation would be destroyed. I will do everything in my power to avoid that situation, no matter what it takes."

Also, when it comes to Brain Training, you've probably been doing things a certain way for many years. You may have turned down speaking assignments at work or avoided making presentations in your business, which has stifled your personal and professional or business growth—causing you to be stuck in ways you may not even be aware of. You might have developed a pattern of avoidance which goes far beyond just avoiding public speaking.

Perhaps you've opted out of singing in your place of worship and missed out on the joy. You might have passed on a toast at your best friend's wedding and missed the chance to do something special for him or her. You may have declined a promotion or shied away from going to the next level in your business and suffered financially and with regret. You've avoided any or all of these things, against your better judgment, because of the short-term physical and mental relief. But it was the long-term pain and sacrifice you may have been oblivious to or chose to ignore.

Every time you escaped from a public-speaking task, you may have felt enormously better—for a while anyway. You've probably trained your brain to recognize that avoidance is not only good, but necessary. Like the best training instructor, your messages were clear, consistent, and repeated frequently.

It's highly likely that what you've thought and done about public speaking for many years, and maybe for most of your life, has increased rather than diminished the fear. You've been Brain Training, and you've done a great job of it. Now, however, it's time to use your Brain Training skills to think and do things differently.

In the next five chapters, you'll learn the Five Stages of Conquering the Fear of Public Speaking that will enable you to train your brain in a different way.

Stage 1—Assessing the Threat and Opportunity
This stage assesses your level of fear and whether it poses a significant threat to your professional, business, or personal well-being. Stage 1 also assesses the opportunities that may present themselves to you when you tackle and conquer your greatest fear.

Stage 2—Preparing for Action
Stage 2 arms you with an arsenal of tools and techniques that will allow you to face up to your fear of public speaking with as much confidence as possible.

Stage 3—Speaking in Levels
In Stage 3, you will work your way through a series of non-threatening speaking opportunities of gradually increasing challenge, to slowly build confidence and reduce anxiety.

Stage 4—Building Confidence
Joining Toastmasters, a nonprofit organization dedicated to public speaking, is the key to Stage 4. Confidence goes up and anxiety goes down as you practice public speaking in the safe, supportive environment of Toastmasters.

Stage 5—Conquering Fear Forever
In Stage 5, you'll take your show on the road, giving safe, fun, and enjoyable presentations to local community groups like Rotary, Kiwanis, and Lions Clubs.

No matter how much you understand about the origins of your fear, no matter how many opportunities you see before you, no matter how much you've internalized the steps it will take to conquer your fear, you still need to make the decision to do it.

Chapter 8
Stage 1—Assessing the Threat and the Opportunity

EVERY DAY THERE'S A SECTION in my local newspaper that lists self-help group meetings. There are meetings for people who fear open spaces. There are meetings for people who fear closed spaces, for people who fear relationships, for people who fear not having relationships, and there are even meetings for people who fear self-help groups.

But amazingly, there are no meetings for people who fear public speaking. This is curious. If public speaking is the number one fear of people throughout the world, why doesn't my local newspaper list meetings for the fear-of-public-speaking group?

There are two reasons: First, people who are terrified of public speaking may be too scared to show up, for fear they'd have to say something in front of the group. The second reason, however, is more fundamental—there are a large number of people who are terrified of public speaking, but who believe it doesn't have any impact on their personal, job, or business lives. They believe it doesn't matter whether they feel comfortable giving a speech, because they think they'll never have to—which may or may not be true. They could be in for a surprise.

Plumbing the Depths of Your Feelings

Take, for example, your plumber who may gag at the idea of addressing a national plumbing convention, but not at the thought of unclogging seven toilets in one day! That's because plumbers don't have to speak to groups to make a living. Ridding themselves of the fear would not bring them more customers.

Overcoming their fear wouldn't lead to greater income for the average plumbers who aren't interested in becoming industry leaders. It wouldn't necessarily allow them to pursue hobbies that they have shied away from, and it probably wouldn't materially affect the quality of their lives in any substantial way. So, they may have no problem living with the fear and see no reason to give up one or two uncloggings just to attend a public speaking self-help group.

As an analogy, I know a couple where the wife is absolutely terrified of spiders. She believes they are lurking beneath every crack and crevice in their house, ready to spring up in the shower, leap unexpectedly onto the kitchen table, or make a horrifying appearance in their bedroom. When they had a deck built last year, she insisted that her husband spray the entire neighborhood with bug spray.

Despite that woman's fear of spiders, there still is no compelling need for her to learn to love those fuzzy, eight-legged, uninvited creatures. It won't make her a better mother or a more effective employee; and it won't open up any new job possibilities. (Well, possibly exterminator!)

People who have the fear of public speaking but can live with it for different reasons are the exceptions. For others, however, the fear severely limits their professional job or business ownership opportunities, impairs their social lives, tests their marriages, hampers their personal interests, and eats away at their thoughts every day.

This chapter takes you through the First Stage of Conquering the Fear of Public Speaking—Assessing the Threat and the Opportunity. The threat represents your personal level of fear which has developed over the years. The opportunity is the proverbial pot of gold at the end of the rainbow—the benefits that will come from conquering the fear of public speaking.

How Do You Fear?

First it is important to gauge where you stand on the fear scale, to determine whether it is manageable—with little impact on the quality of your life—or whether it represents a major roadblock to personal and professional or business growth. I have to tell you there is a quiz involved.

Before you start, however, I promise it's not divided into verbal and math. It's called the Fear-O-Meter, and it contains 15 questions that will test your level of fear and its impact on your life. In filling out the Fear-O-Meter, I have two requests—first, that you don't look over the shoulder of the person sitting next to you, and second, that you answer these questions as honestly as possible.

Fear-O-Meter

Answer Yes or No to each of the following statements.

1. At least once, I have stayed home sick from work or cancelled a scheduled presentation for my business to avoid speaking in front of a group.   Yes / No

2. I have experienced a loss of appetite for more than a day because of an upcoming talk.   Yes/ No

3. If I have a talk to make the next day, I find it hard to sleep the night before.   Yes/ No

4. If I am scheduled to speak to a group, I find it hard to sleep as much as a week before the presentation. Yes/ No

5. I would turn down a promotion at work or avoid striving for a new level of productivity in my business if it involves public speaking. Yes/ No

6. If my best friend or a cherished family member died, I would decline the opportunity to speak at the funeral.
Yes/No

7. Even if I'm passionate about a subject, I would not be able to express myself in a group setting. Yes/No

8. I am uncomfortable making a presentation in front of five or fewer people. Yes/No

9. I've avoided public speaking for more than one year.
Yes/ No

10. I've avoided public speaking for more than five years.
Yes/No

11. Because of my fear of public speaking, I've avoided pursuing a personal interest such as becoming president of my Parent/Teachers' Organization (PTO), or taking a teaching role at my place of worship. Yes/No

12. My fear of public speaking has gotten completely out of control. Yes/No

13. I think about my fear of public speaking at least once a day. Yes/No

14. If I had a choice between instantly overcoming the fear of public speaking or instantly receiving a million dollars, I'd skip the money. Yes/No

15. My life will improve enormously when I can speak in front of groups without fear.   Yes/No

After you have filled in all of the questions, add up the number of Yes responses and multiply by 5; then see how the total fits in with the assessment below. Keep in mind that the Fear-O-Meter is neither a psychological evaluation nor a scientific diagnostic tool. It's simply a way to give you a feel for where you stand on the fear spectrum, and whether conquering the fear of public speaking might make a significant difference in your life.

If Your Total Is 5-15

Why in the world did you buy this book? No, seriously, your answers indicate that you are probably not feeling major discomfort at the prospect of public speaking, and it has not seriously affected the quality of your life or your potential for personal and job or business growth. However, you probably do have some level of discomfort that may not be characterized in the Fear-O-Meter questions.

Although you may not be losing sleep over the prospect of public speaking, you still don't like it, and would rather be doing something else. Nonetheless, you can find tremendous benefit from understanding the nature of the fear described in Part I. You'll find some information in later chapters to help you turn public speaking into a pleasant and even desirable experience—one that you look forward to.

If Your Total Is 20-30

Although you are still on the low end of the discomfort range, you are showing some signs of being ill at ease, and even though it has not permeated your life, the fear has the possibility of increasing over time. You have made a wise investment in this book. It will get you thinking about the snowballing effects of fear, and give you the understanding and tools to nip that fear in the bud.

If Your Total Is 35-45

You are neither completely fearless nor completely afraid. However, the fear of public speaking is making a dent in parts of your life, and beginning to cast its shadow over your personal and job or business life. You know that facing up to the fear, rather than continuing to avoid it, will have a positive effect. But you are not in a crisis mode and could go on dodging and weaving the fear for a little while longer.

If Your Total Is 50-60

No wishy-washiness here. The tentacles of fear are wrapping themselves around many parts of your life and you are feeling very uncomfortable. You are experiencing the physical symptoms that accompany fear and are choosing avoidance over participation.

Chances are, the fear has been building over many years, and you are beginning to feel paralyzed by the thought of public speaking. You're missing opportunities for personal and job or business growth, and are feeling the guilt and remorse that comes from those missed opportunities. For those of you who scored in this category, there is one bright side—you did not land in the next category.

If Your Total Is 65-75

Make no mistake about it; the fear of public speaking has made you miserable. It has a chokehold on you and has the potential to destroy your career or business and personal life. Your body erupts in panic symptoms at the mere thought of public speaking, and you have become an expert in avoiding actual speaking situations at all costs.

In fact, you are desperate to avoid public speaking and will do virtually anything—I mean anything—to get out of it. The fear has taken a toll on your mental, emotional, and physical health, and has worn you down year after year. Something needs to be done—and now.

Imagine What Dreams Can Come True

Now that you have assessed your ranking on the fear scale, it's time to take a look at the other side of the equation—the opportunities to reach your goals and make your dreams a reality that may present themselves to you when you conquer the fear. (You may already have a real opportunity right in your hands that you have not taken full advantage of because of the fear.) These can be powerful motivators for you to take action.

For example, I envisioned several opportunities for myself when I eventually conquered the fear. First, I saw the chance to receive promotions at my job as a communications supervisor to a position as communications manager. The ability to make clear and persuasive presentations is a critical competency in my company, and I was woefully lacking in these skills.

Second, I saw an opportunity to make presentations at local and national communications trade associations, to make a contribution to my trade, and to raise my standing in the industry. And third, harboring a long-time secret desire, I wanted to try my hand at stand-up comedy, to see if I could get up in front of a group and make them howl with laughter (without taking my clothes off!).

Your personal motivators, your dreams and goals, may be a lot different than mine. But it's important to identify them and keep them in front of you as you work through The Five Stages of Conquering the Fear of Public Speaking.

Here's a list of things you may want to do, or do better, as you conquer the fear of public speaking.

Fifty Things You May Be Able to Do Soon
1. Make a toast at a wedding.
2. Participate in a roast at a retirement dinner.
3. Make a proposal at a local township or borough meeting.
4. Present a product, service, or opportunity to a group.
5. Teach at your place of worship.

6. Address your local Rotary, Kiwanis, or Lions Club.
7. Join a local theatre group.
8. Run for local office.
9. Perform stand-up comedy.
10. Teach at your local college.
11. Say the blessing at the dinner table.
12. Tell stories at your kid's play group.
13. Participate in a panel.
14. Call in to a radio or television talk show.
15. Entertain residents of a retirement home.
16. Recite poetry at a coffee house.
17. Read an editorial on your local television station.
18. Join a debating society.
19. Read stories to the sight impaired.
20. Speak up at meetings.
21. Tell a joke.
22. Have your own booth at a trade show.
23. Tell a scary story at a campfire.
24. Give a eulogy.
25. Introduce a speaker.
26. Run for president of your children's school PTA or PTO.
27. Make a presentation about your invention.
28. Address students at your alma mater.
29. Make presentations when asked (or volunteer).
30. Fight a parking ticket in court.
31. Speak to a group of prisoners.
32. Be an auctioneer.
33. Announce a local softball game or other event.
34. Host your class reunion.
35. Defend your thesis or dissertation.
36. Be a guest on a TV or radio talk show to promote a cause.
37. Speak at a training session for coworkers or business associates.
38. Sell management or leadership on a new idea.
39. Host a fundraiser.

40. Perform a magic show.
41. Ask a question at a stockholders' meeting.
42. Entertain patients at a hospital or nursing home.
43. Organize a neighborhood block party.
44. Host a party at your home.
45. Fight for a political cause.
46. Give a puppet show.
47. Lead a focus group.
48. Share your story from stage.
49. Become a salesperson or leader.
50. Become a great salesperson or leader.

These are just 50 of the opportunities that could await you when you conquer the fear of public speaking. There are literally hundreds more. In fact, as you'll see later, the number of opportunities for personal and professional and business enjoyment and growth are nothing short of amazing. But there may still be one person standing in the way of it all—You!

Make the Decision

No matter how much you understand about the origins of your fear, how many opportunities you see before you, or how much you've internalized the steps it will take to conquer the fear, you still need to make the decision to do it. This may sound trivial. You may be thinking, "For cryin' out loud, I bought your book, didn't I? Don't you think I plan to do something about my fear?" I sincerely hope so because it's definitely worth the effort it takes.

Like many people do, making the decision to conquer the fear may require you to make a conscious, out loud proclamation to yourself and others that you're fed up and not going to take it anymore. It needs to be an ironclad decision that you won't let fear run your life, as it may have, to whatever degree, until now. In the 1980s the U.S. government came out with a slogan, "Just Say No to Drugs." Now it's time to make your own slogan, "Just Say No to Fear."

Your firm decision to conquer the fear of public speaking will be a release valve in and of itself. I guarantee you will feel better just by saying it. That alone begins to break the shackles of fear that may have bound you for years.

As I shared earlier, it took me nearly 20 years to come to the decision to conquer my fear. The turning point was seeing my father suffer through exactly what I was feeling. Fortunately, you don't need to wait 20 years to make a decision that will positively change your life. Do it now. Benefit from my mistake.

There are two ways to make and share your decision— privately and publicly. The first step would be to firmly tell yourself, silently or out loud, "I am going to make up for all those years of pain by conquering the fear of public speaking once and for all. I am totally committed to it because I have no reason to tolerate any more pain. I know it can be done; and I understand the enormous benefits I'll reap as a result." Write this down and put it on your bathroom mirror or someplace else where you'll see it every day.

To more solidly state your commitment to overcome the fear of public speaking, go public with your decision. Share it with people who will encourage and support you. They may include   your spouse, boyfriend or girlfriend, your parents, your boss, a leader or mentor, or some friends who'll rally for you and remind you of your commitment.

Coming "Out of the Closet"

Having said that, it really is time to go public. Many of you have kept your fear of public speaking a deep, dark secret. As a result, you have certainly paid a steep price for it in added stress and anxiety—and unrealized success. By keeping it a secret, you have intentionally or unintentionally cut yourselves off from the natural lines of emotional support. Now it's time to remove the artificial barriers you have placed on yourselves, and tell your friends, family, and job or business supporters that you have made the decision to conquer the fear of public speaking.

This public "outing" serves three purposes: First, it will remove the enormous burden that comes from keeping it a secret. Second, it will elicit support and empathy from a wide range of people. Third, it will spur certain other people who also have the fear to admit it and get help.

When I decided to conquer the fear of public speaking, I did just the opposite. I was determined to keep it a secret until the day I could say I was cured. Remarkably, I was able to keep it to myself. But I sacrificed the emotional support and understanding I could have enjoyed from my family, friends, and colleagues. What a shame.

Today, when I tell my story about conquering the fear of public speaking to corporations, organizations, professional associations, and others, I am struck by the level of empathy in the room. People relate to the feelings of fear, desperation, and humiliation I felt along the way. And when I open up the talk to questions, people are honest about their feelings in ways I would never have expected.

So there you have it. You've taken an assessment of where you stand on the Fear-O-Meter. You've considered the world of opportunities that could open up to you. Perhaps you've already and publicly made the decision to conquer the fear of public speaking. Now you've successfully completed Stage 1 of the Five Stages of Conquering the Fear of Public Speaking, and you're ready to begin Stage 2.

One of the most important concepts for conquering the fear of public speaking is to take baby steps.

Chapter 9
Stage 2—Preparing for Action

IN STAGE 2 WE'RE going to prepare for action. We'll be arming you with an arsenal of tools and techniques that will prepare you to safely and gradually test the waters of public speaking.

You'll eventually learn how to speak as well as fish swim. If you're as afraid as I was of public speaking, your heart is al- ready pounding. Just the idea that you'll actually need to stand up in front of people may be setting off your physical alarm bells right now.

But please, calm down. I promise you won't need to stand up in front of an amphitheater full of people anytime soon. In fact, one of the most important concepts for conquering the fear of public speaking is to take baby steps.

Walk Before You Run

When my son, Alex, took his first few steps at age one, he didn't simply stand up unexpectedly, walk out the front door, and stroll around the block a couple of times. He learned to walk after we had given him a lot of assistance by holding him upright, giving him physical support and verbal encouragement, then letting him take it at a very measured and unhurried pace.

With no pressure to perform, or expecting he would run the marathon in a week, Alex one day surprised us by taking six steps from across the room and falling into our arms. From that point on, we watched him as he became less wobbly, more assured, and able to cover greater distances before flopping to the floor.

Just as Alex learned to walk by taking baby steps, you can take baby steps, too, in conquering the fear of public speaking. You need to take no more than one or two short steps at every point along the way. You'll have plenty of emotional support and verbal encouragement at each step, and you'll be able to take it at a very measured and unhurried pace. There will be no pressure to perform or outside expectations placed on you. Just like Alex, you'll be surprised at how soon it will be before you become less wobbly, more assured, and ready to run around the house.

To give you an example of baby steps, let's talk about Jane, who has been terrified of flying and has avoided air travel for more than 20 years. The wrong approach to helping her would be to book her on a very long intercontinental flight, shove her into the plane, hand her a sedative, and wish her luck.

The right way to help Jane would be to encourage her to take baby steps, so she could become accustomed to the idea of flying before ever taking off. If you were to map out a list of gradually increasing challenges for Jane that eventually would lead up an actual plane trip, it might look like this:

1. Drive her by the airport, then drive her home.
2. Drive her to the airport, park in front of the departures area for one minute, then drive her home.
3. Drive her to the airport, park in front of departures for five minutes, then drive her home.
4. Accompany her into departures, stay five minutes, go home.
5. Sit at a gate, watch planes arrive and take off, go home.

6. Sit at a gate, both board a plane. She sits in a passenger seat one minute, gets off, goes home.
7. She boards a plane on her own, sits in a seat five minutes, gets off, goes home.
8. She takes a short flight.
9. She takes a longer flight.
10. She takes a very long intercontinental flight.

Although some of these steps may seem ridiculous to you, I can assure you they aren't to the person who has avoided flying all of his or her life. Even the first step—simply driving by the airport—can start the heart pounding and the pulse racing.

But as a fearful flyer steadily increases the challenges and associations leading up to a flight, Brain Training takes place. Automatic fearful physical reactions decrease dramatically. Ultimately, when the flyer follows the ten steps in an unhurried, measured, rational pace, he or she may be able to fly comfortably to any destination—anywhere in the world.

Enter the Hierarchy of Fears

You can map out a Hierarchy of Fears for just about any phobia—fear of heights, elevators, open spaces, and yes, even fear of public speaking. This is the first and most important tool you will create in conquering your fear—a hierarchy of public-speaking situations that are scary to you, starting with the least uncomfortable at the top of the list and working your way down to the most uncomfortable at the bottom.

The Hierarchy of Fears will serve as your roadmap to conquering the fear of public speaking. Here's somebody I'll call Jack Doe and what his Hierarchy of Fears might look like:

Jack Doe's Public Speaking Hierarchy of Fears

1. Tell a story to my wife and one of her friends.
2. Tell a story to my wife and two of her friends.

3. Tell a story at my wife's book reading club meeting.
4. Present two neighbor couples with a business idea.
5. Present the same idea to these two couples and their two friends.
6. Make a toast at a family gathering.
7. Speak in front of the empty room where my networking organization meets.
8. Introduce a speaker at a networking meeting.
9. Make a presentation at a networking meeting.
10. Make announcements over the loudspeaker at a local theater group meeting.
11. Express my views in front of a local township meeting.
12. Introduce a celebrity at a local fundraiser.

When creating your Hierarchy of Fears, pace the events so that each one is just a little more challenging than the previous one. For example, you don't want to go from making a toast in front of friends to addressing a big convention. If you believe you've made too large a leap between events, think of a more moderate challenge to put in between them.

The Hierarchy of Fears can have any number of steps and, unlike Jack Doe's example, may have many more than 12. Also keep in mind that you can and need to repeat each step as many times as possible until you feel relatively comfortable.

Personal Triggers

In creating your Hierarchy of Fears, it's important to recognize the personal triggers that can set off your fears. A personal trigger is an object, a setting, or even a particular group of people that causes you to have automatic physical reactions to public speaking, such as a pounding heart rate, shortness of breath, or sweaty palms. The triggers for each person can be different.

When I was working on overcoming the fear, my triggers included anything connected with a formal presentation—a podium and a microphone were two big ones. Also, if someone introduced me formally, that was a trigger. In addition, I discovered that having people in the audience who knew me personally was a trigger because I was much more comfortable with strangers. Here is a partial list of potential personal triggers:

- Standing versus sitting
- Sitting versus standing
- People you know in the audience
- People you don't know in the audience
- Podium
- Microphone on podium
- Hand-held microphone
- Tie tack or lapel microphone
- Formal introduction
- Executive, dignitary, or other highly respected leader or mentor in the audience
- Spouse or family members in the audience
- Wearing formal business attire
- Wearing casual attire
- Large group
- Medium group
- Small group
- Applause
- Laughter

It's important to know your personal triggers so you can include them at the right points in your Hierarchy of Fears. For example, I did not attempt to make a presentation involving a podium or microphone until I had made considerable progress in my Hierarchy of Fears. I also found small, intimate groups to be a trigger, so I stuck with larger groups for some time. In your case, if having family members in the audience is a trigger for you, make sure they don't attend one of your presentations until you are further down your Hierarchy of Fears.

So what happens if you inadvertently stumble upon a trigger? After all that careful planning, by golly, there's Aunt Edna in the audience, waving her gloved hand and smiling with those beautiful teeth in anticipation of your talk. Next thing you know, your heart is thumping, your knees are wobbling, and your mind's as blank as a freshly shaken Etch-A-Sketch®. That's when it's time to pull out the next tool in your speaking arsenal.

Suit-Pocket Relaxation Techniques

There are dozens of relaxation techniques. You can play an audio, put on some earphones, and listen to calming sounds. You can sit in a soundproof chamber while a water-pressure machine kneads your back. And you can assume a variety of body postures, in concert with breathing exercises, to induce tranquility in the comfort of your home.

However, if you're about to face an audience of five or five hundred, you may need to have just a few, simple techniques in your suit pocket that are quick, easy, effective, and private. Three of them are: abdominal breathing, muscle tensing and relaxing, and snapping a rubber band.

Abdominal Breathing

What could be simpler than breathing in or out? It's probably no surprise that normal breathing "goes out the window" for someone who is terrified of public speaking and about to face a group of people. If the heart starts pumping and the pulse starts racing, it's nearly impossible to breathe normally without a special technique. Breathing tends to become short, quick, shallow, and high up in the chest. If you start to breathe like this, several things happen—none of which are beneficial.

First, shallow breathing can cause you to exhale too much car- bon dioxide relative to the amount of oxygen in your bloodstream. If you breathe too shallowly, too quickly, for too long, you are on the road to hyperventilation, which is characterized by dizziness, disorientation, a rapid heartbeat, jitteriness, and other unpleasant symptoms. This can lead to a full-blown panic attack, fainting spell, or both.

Even if you don't hyperventilate, breathing from your chest in shallow breaths works against you in the most fundamental of ways. It clouds your mind, breaks your concentration, and disrupts your focus. Believe me, trying to give a presentation without the benefit of your mind, concentration, and focus would not be a positive experience—for you or your audience.

The key to reversing the destructive effects of breathing from your chest is to practice abdominal breathing. Just a few minutes of breathing from your abdomen instead of high up in your chest can produce a deep state of relaxation. It's a powerful technique to have in your suit pocket as you prepare to test the waters of public speaking. I recommend learning to use the following abdominal breathing exercise, reprinted with permission from *The Anxiety and Phobia Workbook*, by Edmund J. Bourne, Ph.D.

Abdominal Breathing Exercise
1. Note the level of tension you're feeling, then place one hand on your abdomen right beneath your rib cage.

2. Inhale slowly and deeply through your nose into the "bottom" of your lungs—in other words, send the air as low down as you can. If you're breathing from your abdomen, your hand will actually rise. Your chest will move only slightly while your abdomen expands. (In abdominal breathing, the diaphragm—the muscle that separates the lung cavity from the abdominal cavity—moves downward. In doing so it causes the muscles surrounding the abdominal cavity to push outward.)

3. When you've taken in a full breath, pause for a moment and then exhale slowly through your nose or mouth, depending on your preference. Be sure to exhale fully. As you exhale, allow your whole body to just let go (you might mentally picture your arms and legs going loose and limp like a rag doll).

4. Do ten slow, full abdominal breaths. Keep your breathing smooth and regular, without gulping in a big breath of air or letting your breath out all at once. This will help to slow down your breathing if you slowly count to four on the inhale (1-2-3-4) and then slowly count to four on the exhale. Remember to pause briefly at the end of each inhalation. Count backward from ten down to one, one number with each exhalation. The process goes like this:

> Slow inhale ....Pause..........Slow exhale (count "ten")
> Slow inhale ....Pause ....Slow exhale (count "nine")
> Slow inhale ....Pause..........Slow exhale (count "eight")…and so on down to one.

If you start feeling light-headed while practicing abdominal breathing, stop for 15-20 seconds, then start again.

5. Extend the exercise if you wish by doing two or three "sets" of abdominal breaths, remembering to count backwards from ten to one for each set (each exhalation counts as one number). Five full minutes of abdominal breathing will have a pronounced effect in reducing anxiety or early symptoms of panic.

Some people prefer to count from one to ten instead. Feel free to do this if it suits you better.

Muscle Tensing and Relaxing

The second relaxation technique is simply tensing and un-tensing your muscles. Now, let's be clear about this. I'm not suggesting that you stand in front of a full-length mirror and flex the muscles in your chest and upper arms. I can tell you (from experience) that it would be impractical and embarrassing to bring a full-length mirror with you to every speaking engagement. I'm talking subtle here. It's a matter of silently selecting a finger, an eyelid, a leg, a jaw muscle, a shoulder blade, a neck muscle, or any other place on your body where you can control the muscle for about 10 seconds.

Let's say you've selected your index finger to start. You simply clench or tighten up your finger for 10 seconds, then release it for 15 seconds. It's important that you focus your attention completely on that index finger and feel the sensation that comes from clenching and unclenching or tightening and releasing.

Feel a sense of relaxation begin to spread ever so slowly through your body. After you've done this with your index finger, move on to another finger or thumb and do the same thing. Clench or tighten for 10 seconds...then unclench or release for 15 seconds.

After you've mastered this technique with your fingers and thumbs, it's time to move on to other body parts. Do your big toe, left cheek, forehead, mouth, shoulders, stomach, calves—even your scalp. The more you practice these simple relaxation exercises, the more your body will trigger the relaxation response automatically. When that happens, you have just acquired an invaluable tool to help you speak to groups of all sizes.

Snapping a Rubber Band

This relaxation technique, also found in Dr. Bourne's workbook, is the simplest of them all—snapping a rubber band between your fingers. It doesn't matter whether the rubber band is between your thumb and your index finger or between your ring finger and your pinkie; the idea is to focus intently on a specific activity. Focusing on the simple snapping of a rubber band takes your mind away from any symptoms of anxiety you may be feeling. This can help keep any symptoms from snowballing into panic.

These suit-pocket relaxation techniques—abdominal breathing, muscle tensing and relaxing, and snapping a rubber band—are tools you can carry with you as you approach each step of the Hierarchy of Fears. These techniques, however, are not the "silver bullets" that will provide you with total freedom from anxiety at every step along the way.

The Hierarchy itself is designed to minimize anxiety. It provides small, reasonable challenges that will help you build confidence slowly and consistently, reducing or eliminating altogether any fear you may have at each step. Having these relaxation techniques available to you can provide additional comfort as you progressively work toward conquering the fear of public speaking.

You've learned how to design a Hierarchy of Fears, how to recognize your personal triggers, and how to practice a few simple relaxation exercises. Now it's time to make sure you tell yourself the right things before, during, and after even the most basic speaking assignment.

Talking to Yourself

Personally, it took me a long time to realize how much the fear of public speaking was driven by the things I said silently to myself in anticipation of a talk. Here are some examples:

- "There's no way I can talk to that group of managers."
- "I'll collapse if I have to face that group."
- "Why is it I'm the only one terrified of public speaking?"
- "I know I'll be awful."

Those seemingly harmless statements, and other ones like them, had a powerful, negative effect on my ability to speak in front of groups. They became self-fulfilling prophecies. If I told myself there was no way I could talk to a group of managers, it was true. I would do everything I could to avoid speaking to that group. If I said I'd be awful, I'd truly be awful.

Undoubtedly, if you've avoided public speaking for a long period of time, you've been saying negative things to yourself too. It's easy to do. But it's just as easy to say positive things to yourself and turn those statements into self-fulfilling prophecies. That's the concept behind The Baloney Sheet—a simple list of negative statements you tend to say to yourself, each statement paired with a matching positive statement. Here's what my Baloney Sheet looks like:

Steve Ozer's Baloney Sheet

Negative: "I'll collapse if I have to face that group."
Positive: "I'll gain confidence by talking to that group."

Negative: "I'm the only one terrified of public speaking."
Positive: "Many people are afraid of public speaking."

Negative: "I know I'll be awful."
Positive: "I know I'll be great!"

Negative: "Oh no, my hands are trembling."
Positive: "It's okay that my hands are trembling; it's perfectly natural."

Negative: "They're just waiting for me to fail."
Positive: "I know they want me to succeed."

Negative: "This is my worst nightmare."
Positive: "This is a fantastic experience!"

Negative: "Everyone can see that I'm horrible at this."
Positive: "Everyone can see my potential."

Negative: "This is the last time I'll ever do this."
Positive: "I'm excited about doing this again!"

Negative: "It's obvious to everyone — I'm weak."
Positive: "I'm getting stronger and better every time—
everyone can see that."

Negative: "There's no way I can talk to that group of
managers."
Positive: "I'm fired up about speaking to that group of
managers!"

Now I'll bet you recognize some of these negative statements, and I wouldn't be surprised if some of the positive ones may seem phony to you. Don't be concerned if you feel uncomfortable about the idea of saying things to yourself that you don't really believe.

The idea is to replace your negative thoughts with positive ones before, during, and after your talk, no matter how awkward, how ridiculous, how phony you feel about them initially. Be encouraged that when you purge yourself of negative thinking, you can't help but feel better about yourself as well as reduce and eventually eliminate the fear of public speaking.

The Exploding Diaper Analogy

Last year we took our kids over to see our close friends, Vince and Barbara Brown, who were having a holiday barbecue for their friends and relatives. Vince had tried to reach me before we left home to tell us to bring swim trunks for Alex, because they had a small pool and sliding board set up for the kids.

But we didn't get the message in time. As a result, we showed up without the trunks and "swim diaper," a remarkable invention that gives kids an accident-free way to swim in comfort, no matter the state of their digestive systems or elimination control.

Of course, when Alex saw the pool, we had to restrain him from running over and belly-flopping in with all his clothes on. So we borrowed a pair of trunks, put on a fresh, regular, super-absorbent diaper...then turned him loose.

I have to admit, those super-absorbent diapers are amazing. After about a half-hour in the water, he had absorbed about one-third of the water in the pool. It looked like he had a basketball under his bathing suit! After about an hour, it looked like a beach ball.

Before too long, it looked like he had blown up into one of those award-winning pumpkins. But none of this stopped him from continually climbing up the sliding board and sliding down into the water and onto his rump with a mighty thud.

Alex didn't know it—and neither did we—that he was now carrying a "thermonuclear device" under his trunks. Although a super-absorbent diaper can hold a ton of water, there comes a point where it becomes totally full. Finally, he went down the sliding board one last time, landed on his rear, and—kaboom!

The diaper exploded. Water and shrouds of soft, fluffy white material were sent flying harmlessly in every direction for a quarter of a mile. We were horrified, but Alex laughed and laughed like there was no tomorrow.

The point of this story is that Alex was having the time of his life with that harmless "bomb" under his bathing trunks. He never worried about what could happen to him or considered the worst-case scenario. He never thought about any potential embarrassment. Alex just kept going up and down the sliding board and having a great time. He wasn't concerned about something that ultimately would do him no harm.

We can all learn from that child-like way of being. Instead of worrying about harmless possibilities, we can open up our experiences to the fun and excitement of the moment. We can replace fear and loathing with enthusiastic participation. We can learn to enjoy ourselves without inventing reasons to dampen our spirits; and we don't need a pumpkin inside our underwear to make it happen!

The most powerful thing about catching your performance on video is that you always look and sound much better than you feel.

Chapter 10

Stage 3—Speaking in Levels

CONGRATULATIONS! YOU'RE READY to begin Stage 3. As we've discussed, climbing the Hierarchy of Fears will allow you to tackle a range of speaking assignments. You'll start with an easy one, then slowly increase the level of challenge at each point along the way.

Remember, you're always in control of the level of challenge and the pace of activity. Again, if you determine there is too great a leap in confidence needed between one speaking assignment and the next, simply think of a less challenging one and insert it between the two. If you need to repeat an assignment once, twice, three times, or more until you feel very comfortable with it, by all means do so.

Before you move from one rung to the next on the Hierarchy of Fears, you complete the following five steps:

- Step 1: Compose Your Own Baloney Sheet
- Step 2: Mentally Picture and Practice Your Presentation
- Step 3: Talk the Talk
- Step 4: Celebrate!
- Step 5: Evaluate Yourself

Step 1—Compose Your Own Baloney Sheet

As you'll recall, the Baloney Sheet is a simple list of negative statements you tend to say to yourself, each statement paired with a positive statement to replace it. To create your own Baloney Sheet, you'll need to listen carefully to the conversation that goes on inside your head when you're thinking about and anticipating each speaking assignment.

You'll also need to think about things you've said to yourself in the past that have caused you to avoid making a presentation or to perform poorly in a speaking situation. Here are five more typical, self-destructive statements you may say to your- self when faced with public speaking:

- "My anxiety will be written all over my face."
- "My heart will be pounding out of my chest."
- "I can't go through with this."
- "I won't be able to take it for more than a minute."
- "I can't speak to that group—I'm a fraud."

By saying these kinds of things, you're only turning yourself into a human pincushion—sticking pins into your self-esteem and self-confidence. Each little prick hurts and, taken together, they cast a negative expectation on your upcoming public speaking performance.

To create your own Baloney Sheet, write (Your Name)'s Baloney Sheet at the top. Make two columns and label them Negative and Positive. On the left, write down every negative statement you've ever said to yourself about your ability to speak in front of a group. Now in the right column, go back and recast each statement as a positive one about either your ability or the situation itself. Let's use the five statements just listed as examples:

Negative: "My anxiety will be written all over my face."
Positive: "Any anxiety I may feel will be invisible to the audience."
Negative: "My heart will be pounding out of my chest."
Positive: "A pounding heart is normal and harmless, and simply doesn't last long."

Negative: "I can't go through with this."
Positive: "I'll be even more self-confident after doing this."

Negative: "I won't be able to take it for more than a minute."
Positive: "It will only take me a minute to feel comfortable."

Negative: "I can't speak to that group—I'm a fraud."
Positive: "No one deserves to speak to that group more than
          do. They really want to hear what I have to say."

After you've composed your own Baloney Sheet, make a couple of copies of it and keep one handy. Carry it with you and practice using it in preparation for each speaking assignment.

Step 2—Mentally Picture and Practice Your Presentation

For a long time, I wasn't much of a believer in picturing things mentally. The idea of imagining something instead of actually doing it left me stone cold. Then it dawned on me that I had been doing it for years. But instead of picturing something positive about public speaking, I had pictured only the negative.

I imagined myself hyperventilating and collapsing on stage. I saw the audience twisting and turning as I stumbled through a miserable presentation, becoming humiliated and de- moralized—running from the stage in a fit of desperation and overwhelming anxiety.

Then I realized, I could change those pictures. I could, instead envision myself winning over an audience with a combination of wit, passion, and self-confidence. I could see myself perfectly composed, self-assured, without a trace of anxiety, delivering a flawless presentation to a group of hundreds or even thousands of people. I could picture an audience that was engaged, informed, entertained, and even moved. I could see an audience giving me a standing ovation, going wild with applause and laughter, shouting for an encore. In short, I could envision a memorably positive experience, rather than an intensely negative one. So can you!

As you prepare to tackle the first rung of your Hierarchy of Fears, and every rung after that, you simply need to close your eyes, empty your head of all other thoughts, and picture yourself and the speaking situation in the most positive light imaginable.

Let's say that one of the speaking assignments on your Hierarchy of Fears is to make a toast at a family gathering—like an engagement party planned for your sister and her new fiancé. Here is how you might have seen that situation in the past....

"I'd like to make a toast."
My words are barely audible, almost a squeak, as I stand next to my future brother-in-law and the punch bowl. I'm not having any luck getting my relatives' attention. They are noisily chatting all around me. I clear my throat and try again...

"I'd like to make a toast."
This time, the squeak is just a bit louder, and I catch the attention of Uncle Jack and Aunt Edna, who turn their heads slightly in my direction as if they've only faintly heard something, and then return to their conversations.

"I'd like to make a toast!"
This time, my voice is quavering and much louder, and there's a hint of desperation in it. Everyone stops their conversations mid-sentence and turns to look at me. My face goes pale...

"I, um, would like to make a toast to my, um, sister, um, Katie and her husband—fiancé—David (embarrassed laughter from the group), and hope that they get everything they deserve (open laughter from the group). I mean, I hope they have the wonderful life together that they both deserve." As I raise my glass to make a toast, the red punch bobs up and down, spilling over the rim of my glass and onto the front of my white suit. The roar of laughter is deafening.

On the Positive Side...

Now, let's picture that scene from a positive perspective:

"I'd like to make a toast!"

My voice rings out with confidence and enthusiasm. Everyone in the room immediately turns toward me with excitement and anticipation, comes to the table and reaches for their glass of punch.

"I am delighted to make a toast to David and Katie, whose announcement of their engagement last week was a memorable and truly happy event. I love and admire my sister Katie so much and I never honestly thought that any man could measure up to my standards and be good enough for her. David proved me wrong. He won me over with his warmth, compassion, sense of humanity, and most of all, his complete and total devotion to my sister and her happiness.

"Looking at them together, it's clear that they were meant to be together. Let's make a toast tonight to a truly happy couple, David and Katie, and to the loving marriage they so richly deserve."

A collective sigh goes through the crowd as they raise their glasses to their lips. Afterward, one-by-one, each relative comes up to me to say what a wonderful toast I had given. You can see by their smiles and by the looks in their eyes that they were genuinely moved by it.

I can tell you from experience that when you envision the positive scenario, you are much more likely to have a positive experience than if you picture the negative one. Once again, it's the power of Brain Training—a simple way to train yourself to see a fearful situation as a pleasurable one.

See for Yourself

In my early public speaking days, I found it extremely valuable to get a firsthand look at the exact location of where I would be speaking. If it was a local hotel room, I would drive over to the hotel a week in advance, ask for permission to see the room, then etch the entire scene in my memory.

I would stand in front of an empty conference table and use all my powers of concentration to imagine people sitting around the table. I would stand behind the podium, turn the microphone on, and listen to my voice booming out through the sound system.

Then, over the next week, I would be able to picture my presentation more accurately. I knew the room, the seating, the sound system, and the acoustics. It wasn't hard for me to conjure up the setting every time I went to practice my presentation.

Practice Relentlessly

Whether you are preparing to tackle the first rung of your Hierarchy of Fears, or the tenth, there is really no substitute for practice. You need to say what you are going to say, over and over, until it becomes second nature. Do you need to memorize it? When you practice it over and over as many times as you need to, you probably will memorize it.

Once you eliminate the fear of remembering what you are going to say, you have just removed one of the major things that can spook you during a presentation. Go back and reread the last sentence. (There is no extra charge for reading a sentence twice!) That, in a nutshell, is why practice is so important. It can dramatically reduce the fear of the unknown to the assurance of the known—i.e., what you are going to say.

Step 3—Talk the Talk

After you've developed and practiced the positive statements on your Baloney Sheet, and imagined and practiced your talk, it's time for the moment of truth—you need to steel up your nerves and face the audience, even if it's for only 60 seconds. It's time for Step 3: Talk the Talk.

Yes, that's right; you now need to do it. Not just think about it, ponder it, consider it, picture it, and practice it. You need to actually do it. When you've followed the steps up to this point and have chosen a first speaking assignment that is only mildly challenging, it's likely you'll have no trouble at all.

Now, that's not necessarily to say you won't experience any symptoms. Since you are obviously not a robot, you may feel at least some of the symptoms you might have dreaded for years, such as the pounding heartbeat, the sweaty palms, and the quavering voice. If so, there are some powerful ways you can reduce the se- verity of those symptoms before and during your talk.

The first way we've already talked about is to use your newly learned relaxation techniques—abdominal breathing, muscle tensing and relaxing, and snapping a rubber band. These are three simple exercises you can do inconspicuously right before your talk to ward off the jitters.

Breathe Deeply—and Care Deeply

Another terrific way to reduce any anxiousness is to choose a topic that you care about deeply. At first glance, this may seem like a silly piece of advice. Of course you're going to talk about something you care about deeply. Why in the world would you be up there in the first place if you didn't?

In reality, however, there are probably only a few people or things that each of us cares about deeply. It might be your family, your job, business, volunteer activities, or your religious or political beliefs. For quite a few, it's your pets.

But whatever or whoever you have strong feelings about, that is what you need to talk about in front of an audience. Because when you feel deeply about something or someone, your mind and heart tends to stay with the subject, you are more prone to remember what you planned to say, and you are less likely to be overwhelmed by fear. Most important, if you don't care deeply about the subject, how in the world could you expect anyone in the audience to care about it?

Periodically, I've been asked to make presentations on subjects of which I may have been knowledgeable, but certainly not passionate about. I've declined every time. I don't think it's fair to expect an audience to listen to a speaker who doesn't have a passion for his or her subject, or at least have a genuine interest. I feel it's fairer to the audience to decline the invitation and let the program director or function planner find someone who is enthusiastic about the subject. The audience will be grateful, and so will you.

"Cue" the Speaker

As a beginning speaker, another great way to reduce the symptoms of fear is to carry a few "cue cards" in your pocket—index cards that distill your presentation, toast, story, or talk down to a series of key words. Be sure to number the cue cards in case you drop them (I'm serious). These are your security blanket if you forget what to say, where you are in the talk, or why you are there.

People tell me they'd be mortified to stop in the middle of a talk, pull out some cue cards, then start back up again. I always ask, "Does the audience really care? Do they recoil in horror? Do they break out in spontaneous, derisive laughter or stand up in a huff, head for the doors, and demand their money back?" The answer is no. Looking at cue cards is no big deal. It's not unprofessional, disruptive, nor uncommon. (One comedian, who performs live and on television, has actually done his entire routine while referring to sheets of paper on top of a grand piano!)

I learned the power of cue cards one night while performing a comedy routine in front of 500 people at a singles charity function. It never occurred to me when I accepted the engagement that single people have better things to do at a singles event than listen to a comedian. I learned the hard way. When I was introduced, above the roar of the crowd, I heard only a smattering of applause, and that was from the lighting technician and the janitor (not a good sign).

Despite the noisy crowd, I launched into my routine confidently, set up the first story, delivered the punch line, and waited for gales of laughter to rain down on me. Nothing. No laughs, chuckles, chortles, or even any guffaws. Undeterred, I plowed on to the next bit—delivered the punch line with equal confidence and achieved equal results. Not only was no one laughing, no one was even listening.

After about ten minutes, I finally started to capture some of the audience, and things started to look up. More and more people were paying attention and laughing. But then it happened out of the blue—my mind went blank. I couldn't remember, for the life of me, what came next or how to get there. If you had asked me my name, it would have been a struggle to remember even that.

In what felt like an excruciating period of time, I paused, reached into my coat pocket, took out my cue cards, found what I was looking for, then put them back in my pocket and went into my next bit. Amazingly, that particular performance was taped for television, and I had the fun experience of reliving my memory lapse a few weeks later when I caught it on TV.

As much as I wanted to close my eyes when the "blackout" happened, I was delighted to see that the entire cue card episode took only about eight seconds and looked entirely natural. The whole thing looked like a natural pause in my routine. It was at that moment that I came to realize the true power of cue cards and of having them hidden but close at hand.

When you use your suit-pocket relaxation techniques, choose a topic you care deeply about, and use those cue cards as a safety net. You will pass your first speaking assignment with flying colors.

Step 4—Celebrate!

Remember, there is no such thing as failure. If you have already tackled step one of your Hierarchy of Fears, no matter what the outcome was, you have succeeded. It doesn't matter how you think you did, if your voice squeaked, if your heart pounded, or even if you lost your place after the first ten seconds. What does matter is that you reversed the course of avoidance that has probably plagued you for years. That, in and of itself, is a remarkable accomplishment. It's time to celebrate.

One thing I love about people is that we all have different preferences, including the way each of us chooses to celebrate. For example, I have an acquaintance who would celebrate by spending a half a day at a health club, taking two aerobics classes, lifting weights for a couple of hours, then heading off to a spa for a manicure, pedicure, facial, and massage.

I, on the other hand, would open a 50-pound bag of potato chips, pour three gallons of dip into a bucket, then lie on the sofa, munching and watching movies from morning until night (just kidding). Still others would spend the day hiking the trails and bird watching at a national park some distance from home or doing something else they enjoy.

No matter what your idea of celebration is, every time you complete a speaking assignment, even if you feel the need to repeat it, go ahead and celebrate. Enjoy the accomplishment with every bone in your body. It may feel a bit contrived at first, but after you've celebrated a few times, you'll begin to look forward to these times when your focus is completely on you.

Step 5—Evaluate Yourself

After you've wiped the chip dip off of your tee shirt, it's time to move on to the final step—Step 5: Evaluate Yourself. To evaluate yourself objectively, assess your performance from the audience's point of view. That's because the audience is bound to have a more empathetic perspective on your talk. After years of telling yourself how scared, unprepared, and unfit you are, it can be extremely challenging for you to cast an objective eye on your own performance.

This is where videotaping comes in. But wait! Before you toss this book in the air and run screaming out the door, let me make a point about the powerful, therapeutic effects of videotaping your performance and watching it by yourself.

Put a camcorder on a tripod in the back of the room or have someone videotape you. This gives you an excellent perspective on what the audience is seeing and hearing. But the most powerful thing about watching your performance is that you always look and sound much better than you feel. Go ahead, read that last sentence again. I guarantee that if you see yourself on videotape, you will be surprised.

This point was driven home for me when I attended that ten- week course for people with public-speaking phobias. My first talk was a three-minute presentation on laser videodisks (something I cared about deeply at the time; go figure). I was scared to death, and remember shaking all over and having trouble catching my breath. But when I watched it on videotape, I was amazed at how calm I looked. You couldn't see my hands shaking, and my voice sounded perfectly normal.

In addition to videotaping and watching it, you need to do two more things to evaluate your performance. First, you need to get the opinion of two or more people who were in attendance. Let each one know you are working hard to conquer the fear of public speaking, and that it was very challenging for you to do what you just did. Then, ask them for their assessment of your performance.

Chances are, you'll receive an empathetic and warm evaluation, which is just what you need at this point. As you become more self-confident in front of an audience, you can solicit a more balanced and in-depth appraisal of your talk, through the use of evaluation sheets, perhaps given to each attendee.

Second, you need to evaluate whether you prepared enough for your talk. Did you capture the right negative statements on your Baloney Sheet? Did you replace them in your head with positive ones? Or did you discover yourself making additional negative statements? Did you say the positive statements to yourself enough times?

Did you picture the setting adequately and frequently? Did you practice the talk as many times as it took to feel comfortable with the content, perhaps even enough to memorize it? Did you choose a topic you were really passionate about? Did you use cue cards? Did you use the relaxation techniques well?

Now is the time to make any adjustments in your preparation, so you can improve your comfort level before tackling the next rung of your Hierarchy of Fears. The idea is to make yourself more comfortable for the next presentation. You'll be amazed at how the process is cumulative.

With each successful performance, your symptoms of anxiety will decline, your confidence will improve, and your desire to take on new challenges will increase. Eventually, you will come to a point when you will be ready for Toastmasters—and you will be geared up to put into action what we talk about in the next chapter.

When I joined Toast-masters I was still a quavering, jittery, skittish pack of misfiring nerve endings. But I immediately felt a sense of excitement by talking with my fellow Toastmasters. I saw the possibility in myself through them.

Chapter 11
Stage 4—Building Self-Confidence

NO MATTER HOW MANY rungs you may have on your Hierarchy of Fears, I strongly recommend that you add one more toward the middle—joining Toastmasters. For me, becoming a member of Toastmasters was the pivotal event in my journey toward pain-free public speaking.

Having gone through Toastmasters' simple, yet powerful, pro- gram, I can see why this nonprofit organization has grown to include 180,000 members with more than 8,500 local chapters operating in 60 countries around the world. Toastmasters has rightfully earned its reputation as one of the most effective ways to fully conquer the fear of public speaking.

As you'll recall from my story earlier, a Toastmasters' club consists of around 20 people who come together to practice public speaking in a safe setting. Toastmasters, as the members call themselves, come from all walks of life. They include administrative assistants, real estate agents, lawyers, ministers, small business owners, accountants, housewives, and people from practically any other arena you can think of.

If you're concerned about whether you'll fit in, you'll be in good company. Practically everyone who joins Toastmasters has the same concern. But, frankly, I've never met anyone who hasn't been taken by the hospitality and sense of fellowship he or she has found at a Toastmasters' club.

There are five reasons why joining Toastmasters is a critical step in the journey toward conquering the fear of public speaking:

1. Toastmasters provides an atmosphere of support.
2. You can see the possibilities for yourself in others.
3. You can practice public speaking repeatedly over time.
4. You conquer fear while gaining invaluable speaking skills.
5. You can remain a member for as long you need or want to.

1. Toastmasters Provides an Atmosphere of Support

Every Toastmasters' club sports a range of public speaking skills among its members. Some are terrified beginners who loathe the spotlight; some are beginning to feel a little more comfortable speaking in front of the group; while others are polished, experienced speakers.

But no matter where members are in their skill development, they all have one thing in common—they are strongly empathetic and supportive of fellow Toastmasters—especially new members. Those who say even a few words in front of the group as part of a formal or informal exercise are greeted with spirited rounds of applause. Having been on the receiving end of that applause, I can tell you it's a nice place to be.

When you speak to a Toastmasters' group, you are in front of a safe, nonjudgmental audience. There is nothing at stake—not your job or business, not your community affiliations, not your reputation, not your self-esteem, nothing. That is an extremely important component of Toastmasters. Since the risk is virtually nonexistent, it lifts the pressure off of you as a speaker.

At Toastmasters, you don't need to be concerned that a less-than-perfect delivery will affect your job or business performance, or your reputation in the community. You don't need to be concerned that people will talk behind your back if your mind goes blank during a presentation. And you don't need to be concerned that people will think badly of you if your speech is less than perfect.

Ultimately, being with caring, supportive people, while having nothing at stake, is a powerful way to set yourself mentally free when you speak. You have the freedom to just be yourself.

2. You Can See the Possibilities for Yourself in Others

Nearly everyone I've met at Toastmasters tells me how nervous they were about joining the organization. Some visited their clubs as "silent" guests several times and could not get up the nerve to join until the third or fourth visit.

Some visited their clubs a few times but didn't return to join for months—or even years later. But nearly everyone is unanimous in telling me that when they did join, they were much more nervous than was justifiable.

The most amazing thing about talking to people who have been in Toastmasters is finding out how much they have changed personally by being a member. I've heard stories about "wallflowers" blossoming into sociable, outgoing, talkative people.

I've heard about people stuck in their careers or businesses who have broken out of the ruts and risen to new levels of success. I've heard about stay-at-home moms who've found a way to add another dimension to their lives. And I've even heard about convenience store owners who went from selling Slurpees® during the day to performing stand-up comedy at night.

When I joined Toastmasters, I was still a quavering, jittery, skittish pack of misfiring nerve endings. But I immediately felt a sense of excitement by talking with my fellow Toastmasters because I could see the possibilities in myself through others. I figured, if someone could sell day-old wieners in the morning and bring the house down at night, I knew I could do the same (bring the house down, that is, not sell the wieners).

If someone could break the logjam of a stalled career and get promotion after promotion, I knew I could too. If someone could learn to make the presentations key to the success of his or her business, I could make the breakthrough I needed to grow professionally as well. If someone else could rid themselves of debilitating fears once and for all, why not me?

3. You Can Practice Public Speaking Repeatedly Over Time

One of the best things about Toastmasters is that it gives you the chance to get up in front of people regularly. You don't need to wait for sporadic speaking opportunities to arise, like your best friend's wedding or your mom or dad's birthday party, to get in the practice.

You can do it at Toastmasters and do it in front of a warm, supportive, and enthusiastic audience. That really is the key to melting away your fears—speaking in front of an audience frequently, and doing it with a group where you feel good about it. Speaking in front of a group that you know won't boo you is a great confidence builder.

I was amazed at how fast Toastmasters helped to ease my fears. After one or two meetings, I was already feeling better about myself. After three or four meetings, I had developed quite a bit of self-confidence in front of the group.

After six months, I considered myself perfectly comfortable speaking in front of that group with a formal, informal, or spontaneous presentation. I couldn't have done it without the ability to practice public speaking in Toastmasters repeatedly over time.

4. You Conquer Fear and Gain Invaluable Speaking Skills

I never joined Toastmasters to become an accomplished speaker. I just wanted to get rid of the fear. But a funny thing happened on the way to that goal. I learned a lot about how to modulate my voice, how to use expressive hand gestures and other supportive body languages, and how to use dramatic pauses.

In the end, I surprised myself by learning how to be a persuasive speaker at the same time I was learning how to be a comfortable speaker. That's the double benefit of Toastmasters. When you stick with it for as little as six months, you have a good chance of becoming not only a confident public speaker, but a good one as well... perhaps even on the way to being a great one!

5. You Can Be a Member for as Long You Like

Not only can you speak in front of the group regularly, but you can be a Toastmaster for as long as you need or want to. I was a member for two years, but gained tremendous benefits just in the first six months. Some people stay with them for years on end, achieving successive levels of Toastmasters' speaking designations, and perhaps even becoming local, regional, even national officers for the organization.

The key here is that you are the master of your own destiny. You decide the pace of your progress at Toast-masters, how long it will take to achieve your goals, and when your goals have been met. The choices are all yours.

I still go back to Toastmasters from time to time as a guest to test out new speeches and to enjoy the fellowship of the groups. I've made lifelong friends at Toastmasters, and I still feel welcomed. If I feel like I need some brushing up on public-speaking techniques, I know I can always rejoin Toastmasters and stay a member until I've achieved my goals and am ready to move on.

What can you expect at a Toastmasters meeting? Although each club runs its meetings with its own degree of formality or informality, there are several elements you can expect to find no matter which group you join.

Prepared Speeches

Prepared speeches are the bread and butter of Toastmasters' meetings. They provide the opportunities for members to present speeches of their own crafting, which they have prepared and rehearsed in advance. The speeches are short, usually five to ten minutes, and cover one of ten different speech objectives as outlined in the Toastmasters' basic speaking manual. Here are a few of the speech topics covered in the manual:

"The Icebreaker"

This is your first four-to-six-minute speech given at Toastmasters, and it has only a few simple objectives: 1) To get you in front of the group; 2) To talk about yourself, and 3) To rid yourself of some of your bottled-up nervousness. Talk to anyone in Toastmasters and they can tell you about their icebreaker.

Everyone's voice shakes a little. Everyone's knees quake a little, and it's normal to go blank for just a second or two. But in the end, you receive a warm and hearty round of applause that leaves you beaming.

"Speak with Sincerity"

The speak-with-sincerity speech is a five-to-seven-minute talk that continues to help you get over your nervousness by having you speak on a topic you believe in deeply. If you firmly believe that mothers need to stay at home with their children in the early years, now is the time to talk about it. If you are firmly committed to the rules of your homeowners' association, make a passionate case.

If you think that building a home-based business can enrich anyone's marriage, tell the group about it. As I said earlier, nothing relieves nervousness faster and better than talking about something or someone you care about deeply. Your focus is on your subject, rather than yourself.

"Vocal Variety"

The vocal-variety speech is a chance to use all aspects of your vocal qualities to make an interesting and engaging speech. In this presentation you will vary the rate of delivery, increase and decrease the volume, change the pitch, emphasize certain words over others, and generally explore different ways to make your voice work for you in bringing your topic across to the audience.

When you start practicing vocal variety, you will begin to see the possibilities of what an accomplished speaker can do. No longer will you see eyes wandering and yawns escaping from your audience, but you'll see clear-eyed attention and genuine appreciation from a captive and engaged group. If you think this is exciting, you're absolutely right!

"Inspire Your Audience"

The final speech in the basic speaking manual is designed to harness all of the skills learned in the prior speeches to do more than inform or educate—the goal is to move the audience. In this talk, you pull out all the stops. Your presentation needs to be clear and well organized. It needs to contain personal stories. The subject needs to be well researched, with compelling statistics to support your argument.

One of the objectives is to use vocal variety to take the audience through the peaks and valleys of the presentation. The audience needs to be moved to take action, inspired to care about something or someone, or angered at an injustice. Inspiring an audience is the highest level of public speaking, and when you get there, you will have truly arrived at a landmark of your own personal development.

"Table Topics"

In addition to prepared speeches, Table Topics are a staple of every Toastmasters' meeting. At each meeting, one member is assigned the role of Topicsmaster. His or her duty is to prepare several impromptu topics and, during the Table Topics portion of the meeting, to call on each member to stand up and speak spontaneously on those subjects.

This portion of the meeting is universally considered the most challenging, but members talk about it in a lighthearted, jokingly sort of way. Table Topics may sound terrifying, but they can actually be a lot of fun. When you practice spontaneous speaking enough, you can become quite good at it.

Imagine the usefulness of the skill of spontaneous speaking if you are stopped by the police for driving the wrong way on a one-way street. You could say, as a friend of mine's father once did, "But officer, I was going only one way!"

Or you could use the skill when your Aunt Gertrude surprises you with a visit on Super Bowl Sunday armed with a truckload of pictures from her recent vacation to a small unexciting place, you could comment, "Boy, Aunt Gertrude, you sure have amazing pictures!" (Amazing is a word some tactful people use if they don't have anything positive to say.)

So, as you can probably imagine, speaking on the spur of the moment can become one of your most valued skills in everyday life.

Speech Evaluations

If you are giving a prepared speech at a Toastmasters' meeting, you'll be assigned an evaluator who will listen to your talk carefully and thoughtfully. Using an evaluation template in the Toastmasters' manual, he or she will make notes on your speech and prepare a two-to-three minute oral evaluation that will be presented at the end of the meeting.

Don't be concerned. These speech evaluations almost always have a positive tone, and are extremely helpful in identifying areas for improvement. In fact, that's where the gold is. The evaluators zero-in on your inherent strengths as a speaker, and target the areas where you can improve for maximum effectiveness.

At first, I used to dread the evaluations because even the slightest criticism felt like a dagger going straight through my heart. But over time I began to look forward to them for their positive reinforcement and valuable insight. Of course, the quality of evaluations varies from person to person. However, you can almost always count on at least one tidbit of information about your manner of delivery or the structure of your presentation that can be quite helpful.

There are several other types of evaluations during the meeting, including a grammarian's report, a timer's report (making sure your presentations don't run overtime), and an "ah" counter's report (someone who dutifully records the number of times "um," "er," or "ah" are said during the course of the speeches). These evaluations are a lot of fun and are always accompanied by playful hoots and howls from the members.

Finally, there are the awards. Many Toastmasters' meetings feature an award ceremony in which members award the first, second, and third-place winners for the formal speeches, drawn from a democratic vote. I still have my award ribbons from those early days. Pleasant memories like these help keep me going; and I can still remember the generous applause from many years ago.

The Turning Point of Toastmasters

For many people, joining Toastmasters represents a turning point in their lives. Mary, the 39-year-old healthcare practitioner, is a prime example. She suffered abuse as a child and was robbed of self-esteem and self-confidence at an early age.

Mary's father constantly berated her, telling her she was stupid, ugly, worthless, and no good. So it's no wonder she grew up with a tortured sense of her own worth and a complete lack of self- confidence. Unfortunately, this resulted in a debilitating fear of public speaking in her adult life.

It was ironic. To her friends and associates, Mary was always seen as warm, enthusiastic, and upbeat. She was someone who certainly appeared to confidently express her opinions—never failing to make a positive impression on people. But behind that happy and confident facade was a woman wracked with fear at the thought of speaking to more than one person at a time.

To make the situation even more challenging, she longed to speak to others who had also been abused—to offer empathy and support and to help them overcome their psychologically damaging experiences. The benefit, however, was that she had a dream to focus on and aim for—something to drive her to overcome her fear. What's your driving dream?

Mary eventually decided to join Toastmasters as a critical step in her journey toward conquering her fear. "I actually called a Toast- masters group about a year before I joined," she says. "But after that year went by, I knew it was time. When I finally made the decision to go, there was no turning back.

"I was really, really nervous," she continues, "but when I got there, I found a warm and supportive group of people." She soon realized that the cooperative, supportive atmosphere allowed her to be herself. She felt she could practice speaking in front of people with no dire consequences and no fear of failure.

Within six months, her results were dramatic. Mary had developed confidence and poise. She had learned how to engage an audience and discovered how to believe in herself. A short time later, she was hired to speak in front of a group of doctors and hospital staff on the subject of stress management. She eventually began meeting with people who had also experienced abuse—offering support and leading them in prayer. Mary wasn't behaving like the frightened little girl anymore. She had taken control of her life, and was determined to give something back to others.

Reversing a Lifetime of Shyness

Beverly, a 48-year-old innkeeper in Cape May, New Jersey, wrestled with an introverted and shy nature in high school—one that held her back from developing adequate social skills. It wasn't until she joined Toastmasters as an adult that she learned how to confidently interact with people, to speak in front of a group without fear, and to show people she had something to say.

"When I worked in New York, one of the men in the company pushed me to join Toastmasters," she says, "and I became a charter member of our company club. I still remember my nightmare of an Icebreaker speech. I was very nervous; my hands were shaking. But after the first speech, I knew I could do it." Beverly began entering Toastmasters' public-speaking contests, and ascended the ladder of winners all the way up to the regional contests—a dramatic accomplishment for her.

Beverly still thinks back to a scene that is etched in her memory, just before she joined Toastmasters, while she was still working in New York. "I was at a meeting with a room full of employees, waiting to listen to a senior vice president talk to us. He had a speech prepared, but I could see that he was nervous.

As he started to speak, his face turned red, his voice quavered, and he started to stutter. Eventually, he couldn't speak at all and had to stop. Here was supposed to be a leader of the company. I knew right then and there that I would not let that happen to me. That's when I decided to join Toastmasters."

From Sedatives to Victory

Emma, 59, is another one who eventually turned to Toastmasters to rid herself of a lifelong fear of public speaking. For most of her adult life, Emma suffered from panic attacks and agoraphobia—a fear of open spaces. Although she was a down-to-earth person who loved people, she still found it impossible to function in social situations unless she was heavily medicated with a sedative. At 57, she learned about Toastmasters and was soon able to face her fears.

Emma attended Toastmasters' meetings every week for two months, but could not get up the nerve to say even a single word. Eventually, she calmed down enough to participate in the meetings, and soon she was giving prepared speeches to a supportive audience. Her progress was steady and sure. Over time, it became obvious that Emma had a knack for public speaking.

A few months later, Emma accomplished the most remarkable feat of her life—she gave a speech in front of 350 people, including lawyers, judges, representatives, and the governor of Oklahoma! The seemingly miraculous change was complete; Emma became a confident public speaker (without sedatives!).

"You Want Me to Do What?"

Amy, the research analyst, first attended Toastmasters at the recommendation of her boss, who had suggested that she needed to work on her communications skills. Amy had never heard of the organization and was terrified at the idea of public speaking. "You want me to do what?" she remembers asking, perhaps just a bit too loudly.

She remembers her Icebreaker as a disaster. "I did the entire speech in one minute and forgot half of it," she remembers with a shudder. "My knees were shaking. There was a knot in my stomach. I was sweating profusely. Fortunately, there were other people there who had given

Icebreakers and had just as much trouble as I did. They were very supportive, helping me feel so much better."

By the very next speech, she was much more comfortable. "I did a three-minute speech and I still had butterflies. But my knees weren't shaking, and I wasn't sweating as much either."

Amy persevered, week after week, feeling her extreme discomfort dissolve into mild discomfort, and finally disappear altogether. Today, she's doing and experiencing things she never would have even dreamed of before.

She reported that, "I took on a leadership role in Toastmasters as District Governor. I taught classes at a local college. I bid on a job at work that would have frightened me away before, and I even started up my own business." Amy attributes this remarkable change in her life to Toastmasters, and recommends it highly to anyone who will get within earshot.

"I Feel Smarter"

Len, a 32-year-old freight auditor, has a unique way of looking at the benefits of Toastmasters: "I feel smarter," he says emphatically. "I used to feel frustrated before because I knew a lot more than I was able to present to people. I've been in the club for more than two years and, frankly, I don't feel so dumb anymore."

Joining Toastmasters, although a critical step in ascending the Hierarchy of Fears, is not the final one. The next chapter takes your new skills and talents beyond the four walls of Toastmasters and out into the big, brave world. But wait! Don't panic! It's not as big a leap as you may think, and it will be your final step in cementing the walls of self-confidence around you forever.

Take a deep breath, 'cause here we go.

Prove to yourself that your newfound comfort is not a fluke—that you can speak to groups of people you don't know, with the self-confidence you've been developing along the way. True leaders care about, inform, educate, inspire, motivate, move, persuade, assist, and entertain others.

Chapter 12

Stage 5—Conquering the Fear... Forever

THERE'S AN OLD JOKE that goes something like this. A man goes to the doctor and finds he has only one day to live. Filled with panic and fear, and overcome with emotion for his wife who will be left behind, he breaks the terrible news.

Then he says, "Honey, tonight I want to take you out for a romantic dinner at the most expensive restaurant in town. We'll eat the finest hors d'oeuvres, drink champagne, and take our time enjoying the fine meal. After dinner, we'll hold each other close and dance for hours to slow love songs. Then, we'll come home and make passionate love all night long. How does that sound to you?"

The wife gets a pained look on her face and replies, "Well, that's easy for you to say. I have to get up in the morning. You don't!"

Anticipating the Opportunity

As much as I welcomed the opportunity to give my first speech outside of Toastmasters, I was still concerned that the audience would respond in a way that was as insensitive as the wife who wouldn't stay home on her husband's last day of life.

I needn't have been concerned though. What I found instead were audiences that were extremely welcoming and supportive of my talks. As I described earlier, speaking outside of Toastmasters to groups of people you don't know is the final step in conquering the fear of public speaking. No longer was I speaking to a group whose members I knew so well. No longer was I speaking in familiar surroundings. And no longer could I be certain of a burst of enthusiastic applause at the end of my presentation.

At this point in your journey, it's time to "take it outside." You need to prove to yourself that your newfound comfort is not a fluke—you can speak to groups of people you don't know with the self-confidence you've been developing along the way.

But where do you need to start? Do you need to book yourself as the keynote speaker at the next National Speakers Association conference? Do you need to gather the staff together at your corporate headquarters for a motivational talk? Or, do you need to check into the availability of emceeing the Academy Awards? Gulp.

No. You need to find a group of people or an organization that would be glad to have you speak for 20 minutes on an interesting topic. More important than your topic, however, is that you need to speak for free, and share information rather than try to sell something. You may think I'm joking here, but there really is a gigantic pent-up demand for speakers in the U.S. and other countries.

Servicing the Service Clubs

Have you ever noticed when you drive into a town, there's usually a welcome sign with emblems bearing the names or organizations such as Rotary International, Lions Clubs, Jaycees, Kiwanis, and Optimists Clubs? Those are service organizations, which exist in almost every town in the world. Rotary, for example, has over 1.2 million members in 34,000 clubs in more than 200 countries, with more than one million members. There are more than 16,000 Kiwanis clubs in 80 countries, with more than 600,000 members. Add in the Lions, Jaycees, and Optimists and you have literally millions of people meeting every week to organize local, national, and international community service activities.

At almost every one of these local meetings, the members invite a speaker to break up the business meeting and add a little pizzazz. You do the math. There are tens of thousands of clubs, many with weekly meetings, all looking for someone to come in and talk to them. You could have a presentation on how to cure Siberian toe fungus and probably find a club that would be thrilled to have you join them as a speaker.

But I emphasize that once again, you can't go asking for a speaking fee and you can't be trying to sell something. The budgets for these organizations are paltry, and they are acutely sensitive to people who are looking for any way possible to get in front of their groups and peddle their services and wares.

What Can You Say?

So what can you talk about? In this environment your best bet is to speak on a topic related to community service. Do you have an idea for a project that could improve your local community, or have you thought about a unique fundraising drive for a good cause?

Have you considered a new and different way for service groups to draw attention to their projects? These types of presentations are surefire winners, and you can be sure that all it will take is one phone call to the program chairman of your local Rotary or other service group to schedule your presentation.

If you don't have the time to do community service, you might consider simply talking about your special hobby. Do you collect tokens from the world's great subways? Are you a great closet kazoo player? Have you perfected an award-winning recipe for fat-free lard? Don't laugh. These topics could get you top billing at a local service organization meeting.

Although these groups are hungry for speakers, don't get the wrong impression of these organizations. I've spoken at dozens of Rotary Clubs, Lions Clubs, and other service organizations, and I am truly impressed with the quality of the people I meet. These are folks who take time from their busy schedules week after week to help their communities. Rotary International, for example, has almost single-handedly eradicated polio from the planet through a concerted global effort.

Personally, I gained a lot of self-confidence from speaking to Rotary and other groups, but I also gained a tremendous appreciation for the powerful impact of their work and for the generous, other-centered nature of their efforts. Go to some of their meetings and see for yourself.

Other Places to Speak

Professional societies and associations are also great places to speak. You may be a real estate agent, file clerk, software designer, administrative assistant, school teacher, an independent business owner, or involved in some other field. You may belong to a professional group dedicated to networking, sharing information among members, and growing together.

Many professional societies have local chapters that meet regularly. When you are skilled at your profession or business and have something to share with others in your industry, you'll probably be welcome to make a presentation at these meetings.

Although the stakes are somewhat higher at a professional meeting than a Rotary Club, it's still a great place to find a receptive audience in a relatively non-threatening environment. To locate the professional society or association that's right for you, go to your local library and check out the Encyclopedia of Associations, or look in your phone book under "associations."

Do you like to garden? Or do you enjoy collecting stamps, cars, dolls, cars, model airplanes, or model trains? No matter what your hobby or interest, you'll likely find a group of people who share your passion. A recreational group is an excellent place to practice your speaking skills.

Because of the fun nature of the get-togethers, the meetings usually are less formal than those of civic organizations, and professional societies or associations. They present a wonderful opportunity to polish your public speaking, as you'll be talking to a receptive audience on a subject you're probably passionate about.

Speaking to a service organization, a professional society or association, or a recreational group is usually a low-stakes opportunity. Your career or business does not hang in the balance. Your reputation in the community is not threatened, and the respect of your friends and neighbors is not on the line. It's the perfect way to test your mettle outside the comfortable surroundings of Toastmasters.

But where do you go from there? How can you continue to challenge yourself, to raise the stakes, to push yourself toward the top of the Hierarchy of Fears? The answer is to speak where you work.

Speaking on the Job

I used to find the prospect of having to speak on the job as a terrifying proposition. I work in a department of communications professionals and each of them is extremely competent at public speaking. Fifteen years ago, the thought of standing up in front of my coworkers made me weak at the knees. Why would I want to reveal a personal weakness for all to see? Wouldn't I be jeopardizing my prospects of promotion by stumbling through a presentation? Wouldn't I be committing professional suicide by standing in front of my colleagues and showing what a wreck I was?

These, of course, are just some of the self-defeating statements we may say to ourselves when we think about speaking at work. However, unlike other speaking challenges, there are some valid reasons to be concerned about speaking on the job.

First, that's where most of us make our living, and it's understandable to be nervous about anything that possibly threatens the consistency or quantity of our paychecks.

Second, the workplace is where those of us who don't venture out of the office as a part of our jobs face the same people, every day, all day. For most of us, we may see our coworkers more than we see our spouses and our kids. So it's with good reason that we'd like to avoid making fools of ourselves in front of this familiar audience.

Third, these are the same people we compete against for better jobs in the company or organization. Our fear of public speaking could be seen as a black mark against us when vying for a job along with someone who is comfortable speaking in front of a group.

When you decide you are ready to speak at work, here are three challenges I would not accept:

1. Try to convince the Board of Directors to change the dress code to formal evening wear.
2. Give a compelling speech as to why your hospital needs a cigar bar next to its asthmatic ward.
3. Attend a union meeting and give a presentation on how layoffs boost quality family time.

Now, to successfully execute a presentation at work, I recommend you consider the following three things:

1. Do It Outside the Realm of Your Performance Review

I'm not talking about accepting a talk that's a long time away from your performance review. I'm talking about selecting a low-stakes speaking opportunity in which your job is not on the line. If you mess up, it won't have any bearing on your review. For example, if your workplace is holding meetings to raise money for the United Way, you might serve as a guest speaker to share your heartfelt testimony about how the organization helped your mother.

This is a relatively low-risk way to introduce your speaking talents to your coworkers. Or you could say a few genuine words of support at a reception for a colleague or associate who is retiring. Neither of these talks has any direct bearing on your review; and no one will grade you when it's over. This will greatly increase your comfort level and chances for success.

2. Choose a Topic You Are Passionate About

I've talked about this before, but nowhere does it make more sense than when you're speaking at work. The examples just given are good ones here, as well. Let's go back to the example of speaking at a United Way meeting.

Perhaps you're passionate about a human services agency they work with that has helped your son or daughter through a difficult time. That makes for a great topic because your passion will help you overcome any initial nervousness. It will also give you an added boost of energy to turn your talk from a ho-hum presentation into a memorable one.

In the second example, speaking at a retirement reception, you may be passionate about the fine contribution your wonderful, dedicated colleague or associate has made to the mission of your organization. If you are truly sorry to see him or her go, you can transform that emotion into a sincere and engaging talk.

3. Pick the Right Time

Timing is everything when it comes to speaking at work. You do not want to put yourself in between your coworkers and something they are anxious to do, such as going to an important meeting, going to lunch, or going home. If you have the opportunity to choose the time for your presentation, choose one that employees might welcome, say mid-morning or mid-afternoon, when many of them are likely to see it as a welcome break.

You may not, however, have the luxury of choosing the time for your talk. Let's say you're scheduled to talk in front of a department after a long morning meeting, just after a huge buffet table has been wheeled into the room. Keep it short. No one has ever complained that a clear, concise ten-minute presentation was too short, especially with a heaping plate of pastrami only a few feet away!

Making It to the Top

If you have conquered one of your greatest fears—speaking at work—you may have reached the top of your Hierarchy of Fears. If so, celebrate! If not, it may be time to look at the top of your list and see if you're ready to tackle what used to be an impossible dream.

Are you ready to make an impassioned argument at your local township meeting as to why the town needs a traffic light on its busy square? Are you ready to share your product, service, or opportunity with a small group of prospective clients or associates? Are you ready to talk to your local garden club about your prized orchid? No matter what's at the top of your Hierarchy of Fears, now is a good time to tackle it.

Chances are, when you're ready to tackle what may have once seemed like the ultimate challenge, you'll also be surprised at how it may not look so challenging anymore. That's the beauty of taking baby steps to climb the Hierarchy of Fears. Each new assignment has given you a manageable challenge, all the way to the top.

Now that you are near the top, the prospect of reaching it is probably not so terrifying. It no longer looks insur-mountable. It's unlikely your palms will sweat or your knees will shake. In fact, in all likelihood, it looks surprisingly doable. It may even make you smile, because you're surprised to see that it's easily within reach. What a treat!

You have all the tools in your arsenal to reach the top of the Hierarchy of Fears. By now, you have used the Baloney Sheet to recognize the negative statements you say to yourself, and have worked to replace them with positive, self-sustaining thoughts. You have harnessed the power of your imagination to recreate vivid mental images of the talks you have given and played back in your mind the positive feedback you've received.

You've pictured the ambience of the room and seen yourself behind the podium. You've heard your voice booming through the sound system and seen the audience visibly moved by your words. You've practiced a few simple relaxation techniques to take the edge off of your initial nervousness, and you've learned to celebrate your success in memorable ways—perhaps with family and friends.

Just Do It!

Now it's time to just do it. Like the mountain climber who needs to climb that final ledge to reach the top of Mt. Everest, you, too, need to take the final step that will put you at the top of the Hierarchy of Fears.

Walk to center stage at your local playhouse, face the audience, and confidently ask them to consider buying a season ticket for the upcoming season. Walk up to the microphone at your son's or daughter's wedding reception and tell the audience how moved you are by the occasion and how happy you are for the special couple. Sit down in front of your child's preschool class and read *The Cat in the Hat* from beginning to end.

Then take a deep breath. It's time to look back at just how far you've come. At one time, the mere thought of public speaking may have set off emergency sirens throughout your body—the pounding heartbeat, the sweaty palms, the quavering voice, the shaky knees. You have now taken control of these symptoms, taken control of the fear, and taken control of your life.

You won't let fear guide your decisions. You won't let panic cloud your ability to speak. And you'll begin to see the possibilities in yourself that have probably lain dormant for years—perhaps even decades.

I knew I had reached the top of my Hierarchy of Fears the first time I stood up in front of 300 people—and bombed.

Excuse Me—Is This Mic On?

I once formed a group called "The Sunday Comics," five stand-up comedians who would do shows to raise money for charity. We would appear at fundraising dinners for nonprofit organizations such as Easter Seals and the American Cancer Society, with each show featuring five successive stand-up comedy routines.

I'll never forget the show where we were asked to appear at a fundraiser for the local police organization. When I walked into the banquet room filled with 300 people, I just had that feeling that something was wrong. However, I couldn't tell you exactly what it was.

By that time, though, I had spoken at enough large events to be able to sense the mood of the audience, just by how they interacted with one another as well as with us before the show. Something negative was definitely in the air there but, for the life of me, I couldn't put my finger on it.

At 8 p.m., the emcee approached the microphone and did his best to quiet the audience. "Ladies and gentlemen, it's an honor to have with us tonight the Sunday Comics. They've made a name for themselves in the Philadelphia area for their fundraising efforts and for their rollicking comedy shows. To get things started, let's give a warm welcome to comedian, Richard Smith!"

This was followed with a bored smattering of applause, and I knew for sure that we were in trouble. As soon as Rich told his first joke, you could have heard a pin drop in the back of the room—it was so quiet. His second joke was greeted by the escalating sound of conversation in the room as 300 people turned their attention away from the stage and back to each other.

Bill Foy went on next, and even though his trademark Irish humor had never failed to bring down the house before, he fell flat as a pancake. Next up was Vince Long, sporting his typical comical sensibility. He died too. Then Fred Fleitz, whose classic comedy style captured many an audience, put up a valiant fight. But, just like the others, his efforts to lower the noise of conversation in the room failed. So, I figured it was up to me to save the day.

Climbing onto the stage with enthusiasm, I thanked the audience for their attention and launched into my first bit. Although there was still some conversation in the room, the audience had turned its attention my way to see if this new comedian would be any better.

My timing was meticulous as I reached the first surefire punch line. I stood back and waited for the howls of laughter...and waited... and waited... and waited. I could hear a lady filing her nails in the back of the room. The air conditioning system sounded awfully loud. I made a mental note of the fire exits.

I boldly shouted, "You've been a great audience!" I then launched into my second bit, certain the crowd would come to its senses. Second punch line...silence. Third punch-line...dabbles of conversation began again around the room. Fourth punch line...the conversations were getting louder. No one could even hear my fifth punch line.

The noise level in the room drowned it out. For the first time ever, I had totally bombed. Knowing when to cut my losses, I stopped mid-routine, thanked the audience with a warm smile, and then ran off the stage. I quickly corralled the four other comedians into the van and headed back home.

In the van, I became filled with an overwhelming sense of joy. My friends looked at me as if I was having a nervous breakdown, but I still couldn't wipe the smile off my face. "Fellas, this is one of the greatest nights of my life," I said, confirming their worst fears about my degrading sanity. "I bombed; absolutely, totally, royally bombed! But it was great! I can do it! I can get up in front of an audience, bomb out, and feel okay about it!"

Fred, thinking I had flipped, was about to call to report the emergency when I grabbed his shoulder and said, "Fred. Don't you see? None of what happened tonight affected my self-worth. It doesn't matter anymore what people think of me. I've finally done it! I've conquered the fear of public speaking forever!"

You're a Winner

Fortunately, you don't have to bomb to feel the way I did. Just realize that it no longer matters how you perform or what people think of you when you stand in front of an audience. Do the best you can with the knowledge and skill you've developed to that point. Sure, you can use valid audience feedback to improve the next time.

But let's face it, when you have the courage to speak in public, you've already done more than the vast majority of the people who rate public speaking as their #1 fear. You are now among the self-respecting few who can say what you mean and mean what you say in front of your fellow human beings.

When you get there, you'll find that you are no longer a follower, but rather a leader. True leaders are the people who care about, inform, educate, inspire, motivate, move, persuade, assist, and entertain others. You're no longer part of the crowd—you're leading the crowd. Isn't that great?

By conquering what may have been your greatest fear, you, perhaps unknowingly, put yourself in a leadership-training program. You're not simply calmer; you're confidently poised to win. You've not simply removed fear; you've added a vital element of success. And you're no longer part of the ordinary masses of followers—you've stepped out of the pack and are leading the way. Congratulations, you deserve it!

When you've tackled what may be the greatest fear in your life—the fear of public speaking—and conquered it forever, everything else is easy.

Chapter 13
Unleashing Your Potential

THERE WAS A TRIVIAL BUT embarrassing incident that happened to me years ago during a business trip. Although I've gotten somewhat better, I still tend to take way too many toiletries and over-the-counter medications with me when I travel.

What if I get a cold while I'm there? I've got cough drops, day- time cold medicine, nighttime cold medicine, nasal spray, sore throat lozenges, vitamin C, and small packets of tissues. Upset stomach? I'm ready with Pepto Bismol®, Tums®, Rolaids®, and about five other products that claim to eliminate those annoying gas pains that sometimes hit after a hearty meal and just before an after-dinner speech. In fact, even if I'm going only a short distance, I travel as if I were heading to a Third World country where no one could understand, let alone pronounce, "Alka Seltzer®."

On a recent trip to San Diego, I had taken a cab from the airport to the hotel. I arrived at the hotel and walked around to the back of the cab to get my luggage. As the driver was handing me a suitcase, the lid popped up and out flew approximately 45 non-prescription medications onto the sidewalk right in front of a group of idling teenagers. It all happened so suddenly. I wasn't prepared for the raucous laughter that came from the group of startled but delighted 15 year olds. Seeing five packages of Gas-X® lying on the sidewalk in front of a luxury hotel was all so funny to them. I've been taking considerably less medications with me ever since that memorable occasion.

I realized that I hadn't felt the naked embarrassment of that incident for a long time until I started to write this chapter. In a way, some of the things I reveal here about myself and others are like that suitcase popping open unexpectedly, depositing all of our secret personal items on the sidewalk for everyone to see.

But before you think I'm going on like a TV talk show host, rest assured that I'm talking about different kinds of secrets—the secret hopes, dreams, desires, ambitions, and needs that lie buried beneath our fears of public speaking.

As I learned about myself long ago, and discovered from interviewing others, the fear of public speaking can fester and grow. It can spread its choking tentacles to other aspects of our lives and suck the life out of our talents and desires that long to be expressed.

For every person who believes they can't speak to a group because of overwhelming fear, there's another who believes they can't be a teacher, a singer, a preacher, a counselor, a lawyer, an actor, a politician, a successful business owner, a daycare instructor, an announcer, or something else they desire to become. We aren't simply mute in front of an audience—we're stripped of our capacity to give to the world what we have to give; and that's the saddest part of it all.

Changing Your Life

If I had to summarize the theme of this book in one sentence it would be this: Conquer the fear of public speaking and your life will change! Because, in the end, being able to stand up in front of a group of people, whether you know them or not, makes you feel comfortable with yourself. And when you become comfortable with yourself, you open up all of the possibilities that have been lying dormant for years.

Chris, a 38-year-old tool salesman, knows what it means to see his life change. At two, he was stricken with polio, beginning a lifelong fear of being different, which eventually translated into a phobia about public speaking. Chris still remembers an incident that happened when he was 18...

"I was asked to speak at a church service," he recalls, "and I remember feeling a tremendous sense of inadequacy. I wondered what I was doing up there, especially compared with someone who was a good talker. I was full of nervousness, overexcited; my palms were sweating. Eventually, I just broke down in tears."

Over the years, Chris internalized his feelings of inadequacy. He avoided public speaking and jobs that required him to speak, like sales and training. Just like the little boy with polio, he had learned to hide within himself. He was afraid of how people would perceive him and whether he would measure up to what he believed was expected of a "whole person." "I lost a lot of opportunities in life," he says sadly.

But, nonetheless, Chris didn't give up. He faced up to his fear of public speaking slowly and methodically, eventually joining Toastmasters in his late 30s. He had a strong determination to get through his Icebreaker, and worked hard on that speech. He was nervous and felt inadequate, but he got through it.

Presenting his Icebreaker was the beginning of a new life for Chris. He slowly began to build his self-confidence speaking in front of groups. In fact, at one point, he had built up enough confidence that when he was asked to be an auctioneer at a fundraiser for a local library, he said yes before he realized what he was getting himself into. "I was so bad that everyone was laughing," he says with a chuckle, "but I had a great time doing it."

Chris had such a great time that he enrolled in an auctioneering school, and eventually held the largest auction ever in his hometown. Auctioning off farm equipment while standing in front of 250 people where he was raised was a miraculous and life-altering event for Chris.

He was no longer the physically and emotionally challenged child with polio. He had changed his life by conquering the fear of public speaking. Today, Chris is a professional auctioneer. He speaks to local businesses and schools about auctioneering, and never fails to recount how conquering the fear of public speaking forever changed his life.

A Breath of Fresh Air

Beverly, the 48-year-old innkeeper, was also transformed by conquering the fear of public speaking. Beverly describes herself as lacking in social skills when she was growing up. She was not part of the "in" crowd in high school. And in college, she was introverted and shy. She eventually gravitated toward computers and a job at a computer services company where she spent more time staring at computer screens than talking to people.

In that position, Beverly's shyness grew over the years until it snowballed to the point where she was literally terrified to face a group of people she didn't know. Her boss at the time suggested that she join Toastmasters, and even though she was scared to death, Beverly still signed up.

As one of her first assignments, she was asked to make a spontaneous two-minute presentation in the Table Topics portion of the meeting. She stood up in front of the room and hesitated for about 15 seconds, until everyone in the room realized she had completely frozen. After a few more seconds had passed, she sat down, paralyzed and completely humiliated. "I have a serious problem," she remembers saying to herself back then.

Beverly remembers the other Toastmasters being extremely supportive in telling her that she wasn't alone—everyone was in the same boat. With their encouragement, she got up in front of the group again and this time found her voice. Over time, her fears began to melt away slowly but surely, and her self-confidence grew in the same proportion. Soon, she was actually leading a Table Topics discussion, giving others the same encouragement she had so warmly received.

Within a year and a half, Beverly achieved the designation of Competent Toastmaster, or CTM. "I saw an incredible change in myself," says Beverly. "The world began to open up to me and I felt like I could do anything. I began to develop leadership skills.

I became an Area Governor of Toastmasters, eventually becoming one of only 68 District Governors in the world." The shy, introverted kid with no social skills had done the impossible—she had changed the very nature of her character by conquering the fear of public speaking. And that was only the beginning....

Beverly ended up working for more years than she'd like to re- member at that computer services firm in New York City. There she grudgingly accepted the fast pace and the impersonal feeling she got from the people in the city.

It was not exactly her first choice of lifestyle, but the pay was good, the experience was valuable, and most of all—the security she felt working for a big company—made it all worthwhile—until she got laid off, that is. The company decided to outsource her department, putting more than 100 people out of work, including her.

Hitting Rock Bottom?

For the former Beverly, this would have been a disaster. It would have confirmed all of the worst feelings she had about herself. But the new Beverly saw this as an opportunity—a golden opportunity for personal growth. She had no idea where it would all lead. The first place it took her was to Cape May, New Jersey, a resort town along the Atlantic Ocean, less than 100 miles from Philadelphia. The warm sunshine, the smell of salt air, and the gentle ocean breezes welcomed her.

But it was the beautifully appointed Victorian homes and businesses, as much as the balmy weather, that caused Beverly to fall in love with Cape May. With just one visit, she knew she had found the place to make a dramatic career change—and enjoy the rest of her life.

Scraping together the money she had saved for years, Beverly bought an old Victorian home in Cape May. After major renovations, it was transformed into a comfortable and cozy inn, one of the many "bed and breakfast" places that dot the Cape May coastline.

Drawing on her newfound people skills that had come from conquering the fear of public speaking, Beverly became active in the community. She began networking with other business owners and joined the local Chamber of Commerce. Within a year, she came to be known as a leader in Cape May—a gifted and eloquent spokesperson for small-business establishments.

For Beverly, the change in herself and her life was nearly miraculous. She had graduated from a shy and introverted teenager to a respected community leader within a matter of a couple of years. Conquering the fear of public speaking was the key to changing her life.

Tapping the Well of Self-Confidence

Amy, the research analyst whose struggle you learned about earlier, also changed her life in an exciting way by conquering the fear of public speaking. For years and years, Amy was tortured not only by the thought of speaking in front of groups, but also by the thought of being with her husband. His attitude and behavior toward her was insensitive, cruel, and abusive. When she finally took the steps necessary to conquer the fear of public speaking, he was, to put it kindly, less than supportive.

Amy suffered a double whammy in her efforts to conquer the fear. She fought the terrible plague of doubt within herself, while suffering the heartless and callous abuse from a husband who would have been happy to see her fail in the most important challenge of her life.

As you'll recall, Amy did manage to conquer the fear of public speaking, and as we saw with Chris and Beverly, she also saw her life change dramatically for the better. But there was still the matter of her husband, whose attitude and behavior hadn't changed.

By conquering the fear of public speaking, Amy tapped into a well of self-confidence even she didn't know she had. Eventually, she began to wonder why she had ever allowed her husband to put her down in the first place. Moreover, she still loved him and was determined to do whatever it took to make the relationship work.

Consequently, she expressed her feelings and miraculously managed to get him to go to marriage counseling—which she wouldn't have had the self-esteem to do before. It was a challenge, to say the least. But she's happy to report that after extensive counseling, they finally have a great relationship. They're even planning a family! By successfully working on their marriage, Amy had cast off the final weight that had held her down in life. Now, anything was possible.

What About Other Fears?

I was speaking to a writers' group recently about these experiences when a woman asked me a very good question: "How can I be sure that after conquering the fear of public speaking, some other fear won't simply rise to the surface and take its place?" I acknowledged her concern and pointed out that because the fear of public speaking can be so large and overwhelming, it can often cover up other fears that lurk beneath it.

But there's a big, big difference. When you've tackled what may be the greatest fear in your life and conquered it forever—the fear of public speaking—everything else is easy.

I'll give you the strongest example from my own experience. After I conquered the fear of public speaking, I felt like Superman. I was doing things I never dreamed possible—standup comedy, after-dinner speeches, wedding toasts, and more. It also became crystal clear to me for the first time that, although I was now comfortable speaking in front of groups, I was still lonely. I was lonely because of another pervasive fear—the fear of commitment.

Actually, I had become a serial relationship builder. Each of my relationships with women would last about three years or so, then I would invariably start to feel enveloped, smothered, shut-in, and trapped. I didn't realize it at the time, but I was suffering from the fear of commitment.

Just when it was time to think about making a more formal commitment—getting engaged or simply talking about the possibility of marriage—I would get panicky and begin to unconsciously sabotage the relationship. I'd become moody and demanding. I'd find fault with her. I'd withdraw.

Inevitably, my girlfriend would break up with me, and although I'd brought it on myself, I'd always let myself be destroyed by it. I'd realize how much she meant to me. I'd beg her to come back. I'd go into a depression. Then, in the end, I'd end up lonely once again, ready to start the cycle of pleasure and pain with a new relationship.

After conquering the fear of public speaking, I recognized the fear of commitment in myself and saw it for the phobia that it was. In many ways, it was like claustrophobia—the fear of enclosed spaces—in which the relationship itself would seem to suffocate and trap me until

I simply had to get out. Finally, after all those painful years of suffering from commitment phobia, I now had the skills and experience to conquer it once and for all.

At that time, I hadn't developed an action plan that would be- come the basis for this book. But I did understand that my fear of commitment would have to be overcome in a series of baby steps. Even then, I had a rough idea in my mind of what the Hierarchy of Fears would look like:

Commitment Phobia Hierarchy of Fears
1. Meet someone I really like.
2. Begin to date regularly.
3. Begin to date exclusively.
4. Discuss marriage as a distant possibility.
5. Discuss marriage as a real possibility.
6. Discuss possibility of having kids.
7. Discuss getting engaged.
8. Get engaged.
9. Plan wedding ceremony together.
10. Get married.
11. Discuss timetable for having kids.
12. Have kids.

I realize that reading this off the page may sound very clinical to you or even silly. But when the time came for me to put the theory into practice, our relationship simply progressed the way any normal one would—but without anxiety.

Goodbye Fear, Hello New Life
When I look at the pictures of my two beautiful kids on the refrigerator, I see the most powerful result of what conquering fear can do. For me, conquering fear meant bringing new life into the world. For you, it may mean finding a new job or profession, building a business, pursuing an artistic vision, standing up for your rights,

healing a hurtful relationship, giving to the community, leading a group in prayer, enjoying a life of public service, or simply captivating a group of children with an engaging story.

Too many of us, consciously or unconsciously, resolve to live with fear and never find the key to true happiness. We look for fulfillment in other ways—by having more things, by finding different relationships, or by increasing our social standing.

True happiness, however, can often be found within ourselves, locked away behind the iron gates of fear. By finding the courage to unlock those gates and release the fears that have suffocated us for so long, we can breathe the fresh air of life lived to the fullest. I did it and you can too.

Now go for it—I dare you! Overcome your fear of public speaking and a whole new world will open up for you.

"**B**e of good cheer. Do not think of today's failures, but of the success that may come tomorrow. You have set yourself a challenging task, but you will succeed when you persevere; and you will find joy in overcoming obstacles. Remember, no effort that we make to attain something beautiful is ever lost."

—Helen Keller

Who Is Steve Ozer?

Steve Ozer worked in communications and public relations more than 20 years for one of the world's premier specialty chemical companies. He's also the past president and founder of Powerful Public Speaking, Inc. Since conquering a debilitating fear of public speaking, Steve has spoken at national conferences, performed in comedy clubs, and appeared on television and radio. However, most importantly, he has brought his message of empowerment in conquering the fear of public speaking to thousands of other people.